Advance Praise for *Black Liturgies*

"Cole Arthur Riley is a spiritual guide and a gift in our lives. Restoring us to ourselves and reminding us of our humanness, our fragility, and the strength of faith, she calls us back to community, to breath, to our god-given selves. *Black Liturgies* is true spiritual balm for our troubled times."
—MICHAEL ERIC DYSON, PhD,
New York Times bestselling author of *What Truth Sounds Like*

"*Black Liturgies* is a garden for the soul. With rare wisdom, beautiful clarity, and generous vulnerability, Arthur Riley brings her whole self to these letters, verses, and promptings, offering bright, deep truths about who we are and can be as Black women, Black people, and human beings. Hold these luminous words close and let them be your balm."
—TIYA MILES, PhD,
National Book Award–winning author of *All That She Carried*

"Cole Arthur Riley is a blessed seer and curate. In *Black Liturgies* she nurtures souls, hearts, and intellects through storytelling, prayer, and deep reflection. Readers will be deeply moved by the beauty of her writing and her moral clarity, tenderness, and wisdom. This is a book to cherish and share."
—IMANI PERRY, PhD,
National Book Award–winning author of *South to America*
and columnist at *The Atlantic*

"This is a curation of musings that renders the Spirit accessibly real— not up in the 'heavens' or beyond our reach, but right here within. In our hands, we hold a sacred Blackness. *Black Liturgies* will quiet you and guide you into the limitless space of your self."
—YABA BLAY, PhD,
cultural worker and author of *One Drop: Shifting the Lens on Race*

"Cole Arthur Riley continues to show that she is one of this time's most powerful and potent writers on the body and spirit. What she shares is at once quiet and honest, intimate and profound. The prayers in this book seem to rise from our own cracks and breaks, from the deep well of Blackness itself. They remind us to pray only to the God that could know us and love us, and that intended us to be this beautiful and this human."

—PRENTIS HEMPHILL, author of *What It Takes to Heal* and founder of the Embodiment Institute

By Cole Arthur Riley

This Here Flesh
Black Liturgies

BLACK
LITURGIES

BLACK LITURGIES

PRAYERS, POEMS, AND MEDITATIONS

FOR STAYING HUMAN

COLE ARTHUR RILEY

CONVERGENT

New York

Published in the United States by Convergent Books,
an imprint of Random House, a division of Penguin Random
House LLC, New York.

Permissions credits are located on page 305.

LIBRARY OF CONGRESS CATALOGING-IN-PUBLICATION DATA
Names: Arthur Riley, Cole, author.
Title: Black liturgies / Cole Arthur Riley.
Description: First edition. | New York : Convergent, [2024] |
Includes bibliographical references.
Identifiers: LCCN 2023034028 (print) |
LCCN 2023034029 (ebook) | ISBN 9780593593646 (hardcover) |
ISBN 9780593593653 (ebook)
Subjects: LCSH: African Americans—Religious life. |
African Americans—Prayers and devotions.
Classification: LCC BL625.2 .A79 2024 (print) |
LCC BL625.2 (ebook) | DDC 248.8089/96073—dc23/eng/20231002
LC record available at https://lccn.loc.gov/2023034028
LC ebook record available at https://lccn.loc.gov/2023034029

Printed in the United States of America on acid-free paper

convergentbooks.com

8th Printing

First Edition

Book design by Fritz Metsch

The authorized representative in the EU for product safety and
compliance is Penguin Random House Ireland, Morrison
Chambers, 32 Nassau Street, Dublin D02 YH68, Ireland.
https://eu-contact.penguin.ie.

For us.

Contents

PART TWO: BY TIME

Entrance

I NEVER wanted to write a prayer book. I grew, and my love for writing grew, at a great distance from Christian literature of any kind. By the time I was in college, I had developed enough of a palate (and arrogance) for what I deemed "serious" literary fiction that I would find myself internally wincing at book recommendations in the church I'd begun attending. The same suspicion I felt toward their God was mapped onto his alleged scribes. I believed (and still largely do) that the most trustworthy, and perhaps meaningful, literature can be found in the economy of the short story, the nuance of the memoir, the imagery of the poem. Literature—real art—could not be found in a church pew; how could it? Religion's purpose is to bring mystery close enough to touch. We give God a name, a face. We write creeds to outline the conditions of our belief. This requires that the mystery stay still and at times contract. But art has little concern for definition, certainty, or even permanence; it survives by the mystery expanding and re-creating itself. In *Parable of the Sower*, for example, Octavia Butler is not interested in telling you *what* precisely to believe about Lauren's desire to leave the walled neighborhood in the middle of apocalypse. She only cares if you rise and go on the journey.

Lucille Clifton put it, "You come to poetry not out of what you know but out of what you wonder." It is conveyance, rarely indoctrination. In this way, good art is necessarily queer—fluid and subversive and impermanent. Religion, stripped of such queerness, can be excessively clear and uncompromising in its rigidity. But when practiced well, religion—or more broadly, spirituality—has the capacity to tether incomprehensible mystery to the beauty and pain of the human heart. It is not the only way to do so, but it is one way.

To be a writer with any sincere concern for the human condition as we've known it, one must contend with the spiritual. This is inescapable. The question, I suppose, is one of form. I want a mystery that contracts so that I can dare approach, that I can turn over in the palm of my hand but then watch pass through my fingers and become the air I breathe. I want a spirituality that demands artistry, not just from the divine but from me. All of this has required me to interrogate if I believe the form of liturgy has any merit. As you are reading these words, you can rightfully assume I've come to the admission that it does.

I was twenty-three when I walked into an Episcopal church with an overwhelming desire to die. The service began with a hymn. Two dozen elderly choir members hovered above us from the loft, singing words I couldn't make out, which has its own way of making you feel alone. But then all around me people began to speak the liturgy aloud. *Blessed be God. And blessed be God's kingdom, now and for ever.* As the voices began their recitation, a few things occurred in me at once. First, defiance—the atoms of me surged in resistance. To recite words like some mindless zombie? I had my own thoughts, my own idealized individualism to protect. The second, chills. The voices of the room blurred together, all speaking in unison. How strange this landed on the senses. What cult was this? Liturgy can feel eerie, especially to those of us who know what it is to have a mob chant words in unison, not for beauty or mystery, but for destruction. But the third, relief—complicated and undeniable relief. It can be difficult to find the words to pray when one wants to die. The independence of personal prayer required more imagination than I could access at the time. It is exhausting enough trying to keep oneself alive; to be expected to articulate love and hope and beauty—and more dangerously, lament—was like trying to float with weights hanging from my neck. Liturgy, I found, was a kind of rest. For the first time, my presence in a spiritual space didn't depend on my own articulation or imagination. I could rise and sit and kneel and speak or not speak in this sacred theater that others had written the script for. I could let others hold a sacred imagination for me.

To be clear, liturgy in no way saved me, nor was it even a remedy to my depression. But it was an anchor, something that kept me from drifting helplessly into my own interior current. Ritual, when coupled with beauty, makes for a very adequate mooring. It won't carry you to shore, but it will keep you close enough that hope can swim out to visit you regularly.

Years later, in the summer of 2020, I began a project called Black Liturgies. It was a season when many wondered if the world might be prepared to at last contend with the terror of whiteness armed against Black bodies. We witnessed brutal public executions. Elijah McClain was taken from us. Ahmaud Arbery. Breonna Taylor. And then George Floyd, and non-Black people weren't as quick to look away (or so it seemed). For Black folk, nothing of this was new, of course. Before Breonna, there was Sandra Bland. Before Elijah, there was Tamir Rice. Before George, there was Eric Garner. But with the awakening of white attention came white opinion, and a white president who stoked racial divisions at the site of religious fault lines.

As people began to reveal their moral allegiances, many Black people experienced renewed gratitude for spiritual spaces capable of holding their grief and hope. Others looked around and realized we weren't as safe in church as we thought we were, as many white evangelical spaces revealed precisely who they've always been to queer people, disabled people, refugees, immigrants, Black people, and other people of color. The exodus from toxic religiosity became more urgent for many of us. Coupled with the isolation of the pandemic, the search for more honest and creative spiritual community was awakened in a new way.

The Sunday after George Floyd's murder was Pentecost Sunday. While still in the height of the pandemic, I logged into an Episcopal church service online and waited for some manner of belief to return to me. I lay in the same position I had been for days prior, a cluster of grapes and a bag of hot Cheetos on the pillow next to me. And I waited, knowing what I've always known: that there are days when it is particularly difficult to pray words written by a white man. For all its beauty, this liturgy that had given me words to pray when I had none was suffocating. Thomas Cranmer, who wrote the Book of Common Prayer at a time when my ancestors were being abducted, alienated from one another, and enslaved, would not be an anchor for me that day. He was incapable of speaking to my pain, Black grief, Black hope, in a voice I could trust. I wanted more.

And so I began Black Liturgies. Mostly out of rage. I cannot say how much of my rage was holy and how much was hatred, but I hope it contained more of the former. I was desperate for a liturgical space that could center Black emotion, Black literature, and the Black body unapologetically. I began sharing poetry and prayers and quotations on social media. I thought the project would bring together a dozen or so of us who weren't in physical proximity to one another but maybe were craving the same thing—space to breathe. I watched the project quickly become a community of many more—people who love liturgy and people who had never even heard the word. Christians *and* people who had never set foot in a church. It is a space held together by the sacredness of Black words alone.

When I write, I try to be transparent in naming that I am writing out of a Christian formation. I've found meaning and beauty in the Christian story, and I honor that. However, I am equally transparent in naming that my spirituality cannot be reduced to this. I was not raised in an overtly religious home, but as I've gotten older, I've been able to decipher the discrete presence of spirituality that flows through my family—a spirituality grounded not in articulation of doctrine or creed, but in storytelling, myth, humor, and the Black body. And so, while some of these liturgies will speak to a Christian spiritual formation, others will speak to a Black spirituality, others to a queer spirituality, others a mythical spirituality. These are, of course, not mutually exclusive, but this is to say that if this book has loyalty to anything, it is to spiritual liberation in all its incarnations and complexities. Whatever spirituality calls to you from these liturgies, I hope it leaves you feeling more free. To believe or not believe. To feel what you feel. To be free in your body. And still, as the words of this book are tethered to me, an individual, I must warn of the limits in its diversity. There are places in you, I'm certain, I have failed to locate words for, corridors of the heart that I have not walked.

My hope is that an array of people will approach these pages, however suspiciously or cautiously. That they might serve as a harbor for those who have escaped the trauma of white Christian nationalism, religious homophobia and transphobia, biblical ableism, and ecclesial misogyny; those healing from spiritual spaces that were more violent than loving, more tyrannical than liberating.

The Greek origins of the word *liturgy* can be translated to "work of/for the people." Most simply, it is a form for a sacred experience, often practiced in community and habitually. The ceremony of a Catholic or Anglican rite are examples that often come to mind, but liturgy is far more universal than even these spiritual expressions. Throughout space and time, peoples have imagined and reimagined forms for communing with the divine or revering the sacred, be it an altar to the ancestors, the recitation of Mussaf on Shabbat, the Okuyi practiced by some Bantu groups, or the artistry of Tai Chi. Liturgy may contain prayer, but it is certainly not synonymous with it.

The liturgy that I've found healing in happens to be written liturgy. For me, reimagining written prayer outside of the white gaze has been a practice in both liberation and solidarity. Something striking happens when you are made to read words written in particularity, with a shared voice. All of a sudden you may come across a phrase or an emotion that doesn't immediately resonate with you. It may not be *for you*. But what does it mean to commit yourself to staying in the room—remaining in the words even if they don't immediately speak to you? Are you capable of decentering yourself long enough to hear the voice of another? Will you take up the words alongside them, never overpowering them but following in solidarity? And it is a practice in liberation, as I am brought home to my own interior world. There, I am liberated into emotion. Rested in my body. I am brought near to self, neighbor, ancestor, and the divine in a ritual that feels safe and honest.

I cannot promise you that this form of liturgy is your path, that it will feel like a homecoming for you, that it will restore your faith. The truth is that it is not for everyone. Still, receive this invitation. I do not need you to have the same experience with the sacred as I have, but I'm quite interested to see if you'll rise and come on the journey. It is not lost on me that I am asking you to trust me as an adequate guide, and I should tell you that most days I feel like I'm wandering. I am working on my sense of direction. But my promise to you is that every word in this book has been written, interrogated, and preserved with an imagination for collective healing, rest, and liberation. And any mystery within these pages certainly cannot be contained to them. These are only fragments of divine encounter, and I am proud of that. Turn them over in your hand. Take a deep breath.

Architecture

I'VE CONSTRUCTED this book in two parts. Part One, "By Story," is concerned with the existential—the shared questions and longings of the human experience. Grief, Delight, Remorse, Belief. How can we find a resting place in the disparate conditions of existence? And how is the spiritual enmeshed with these questions and longings? The letters and liturgies in this section can be approached with a kind of dailiness, but dependent on and in reflection of your circumstances or interior life. These can, of course, be read in both community and solitude—in whatever company the words appear most true. Some phrases move differently when you aren't glancing over your shoulder. Others can only be sustained with the arms of another holding you up.

Part Two, "By Time," is organized around the temporal—our relationship to the divine in respect to time. Be it the hours of the day or particular seasons or days of observance, this is where habit and cycle live in the book. What are the rhythms that hold together one's spiritual life? What are the celebrations and laments written into our years? There are liturgies for church holidays, for occasions such as Juneteenth, Mother's Day, Kwanzaa; as well as morning, midday, and evening prayer. Not all seasons or days given space in these pages will resonate or be observed by all. There are, for example, a number of sections grounded in a Christian liturgical calendar. There is a liturgy for a homegoing service, which is distinct from what others would consider a mere "funeral." Whatever the page, enter and depart as feels right and true for you and the community you practice within.

The book is held together by several core elements:

ANCESTORS—To encounter the spiritual absent from the dead, absent from the people who made us, is no longer a risk I am willing to take. Each section will include quotations or excerpts from Black ancestors. Some are writers, artists, leaders of social movements. I cannot do this work without their guidance and instruction. We possess the privilege of time; with each generation, there is an increase in our access to the wisdom of those who came before us. It would be irresponsible of me to create a liturgical artifact without them. You'll also find quotes from the land of the living—people whose words I expect will stretch far into time.

LETTERS—Letter writing is a dying art, and I've been trying to resurrect it in my own relationships. It's a very humbling practice, especially by hand, as you don't have the same freedom in editing that you do in a text or an email. You hurriedly go to cross out a line, but the page will not soon forget the error. I am also, of course, confronted with my own penmanship, which can feel very cruel. I live with a few neurological conditions that have made fine motor movements difficult, and my handwriting now appears to me rippled and rugged and imprecise. Letters have been a reminder, however welcome or not, of my own mortality. And a puzzle of legibility at times, though for you I've typed them.

But in all, I've found that the pen changes when it's writing *to* someone as opposed to *for* someone. You aren't writing to prove a point, but to relay your inner world in the way you need to on that particular day. The next morning you might wake to find it not so big of a deal that you burned your dinner the night before. But the letter lives on, unapologetic in its drama.

And in a world where we are consistently force-fed narratives about our own indignity, about the everyday realities of the oppressed, about the unquestionable heroism of those in power, letter writing can be a form of resistance. Say your own thing and say the thing your way and say it without those who might destroy you peeking over your shoulder. Throughout history, we have sought ways to communicate unintimidated by the propaganda of an oppressive society. The letter is closer to the silent nod of two people passing by each other on a dimly lit sidewalk than it is to any dissertation. This is how we rally and decolonize and liberate our interior worlds. We hold on to one another, eye to eye, as we tell a truer story. It is preservation.

POETRY—The heart of the liturgist is near to the heart of the poet. In terms of the human experience, each is responsible not for teaching but for expressing—however inconclusive or raw that expression may be. But liturgy is just nearly poetry, never quite. It lacks an intentional shape on the page, it lacks poetic structure, and it often becomes wordy where poetry is more economical. Perhaps liturgy is the verbose sister of the far more discriminating art. Neither need apologize for their distinct qualities. And there is something to be said for the fact that many spiritual writers throughout history have also been poets.

What does it mean to be formed by poetry? To adhere to the rhythm, to surrender to every line break, to be present to the sensory? The ancients understood what James Baldwin later asserted: "The poets (by which I mean all artists) are finally the only people who know the truth about us. Soldiers don't. Statesmen don't. Priests don't. Union leaders don't. Only poets." And so, throughout these liturgies, I've tried to access the heart of a poet in me to convey a kind of truth. While I've written many of the poems you'll encounter in this book, I should say the poet's voice is distinct from the voice of the letter writer, which is definitively mine. In the poems, if there is an "I" present, you can rightfully assume it is not me. On the rare occasion I do appear, it is in fragments. What is critical is that you locate someone real in the words, preferably yourself. As Helen Vendler put it, "You don't read or overhear the voice in the poem, you are the voice in the poem. You stand behind the words and speak them as your own."

BREATHE—When I first began attending Episcopalian and Catholic services, I was stunned to discover what the liturgy required of my body. Standing, sitting, kneeling, bowing, gestures and postures, the smell of the incense, the bread, the wine. It was an incredibly sensory, corporeal engagement. And it connected me to the physical in ways I couldn't anticipate. This was no disembodied, invisible, spiritual encounter; this ritual was living in the body. And it was not just about the power of the body, but the frailty. There were days when my limitations were inescapable. Could I endure the cold wood of the kneeler digging into my wobbly knees as I mumbled my confession? How much longer could I stand before my muscles began to twitch? Am I well enough to attend at all? Can I breathe the air and not be destroyed?

I've belonged to spiritual spaces that required I forget my body—my Black, woman, sick body—to survive. I want the liturgies of this book, and any spiritual encounter, to make me more whole, never dismembered. And so I've included breath prayers with each liturgy, as a reminder and practice of that. Will we breathe together? Relax our shoulders, unclench our jaws? For the divine is just as present in our breath, in our flesh, as in our mental realm.

CONFESSION AND FORGIVENESS—Confession is a ritual that draws us toward the reflection and self-honesty that often escapes us in our daily lives. June Jordan wrote, "To tell the truth is to become beautiful, to begin to love yourself, value yourself. And that's political, in its most profound way." What does it mean to become a truth-teller, to encounter your own face and not look away? Who is saved by our admissions of guilt? Confession, as an anti-delusion practice, saves its utterer far more than the wounded. It is not repair, only its preface. But this does not make its honesty any less necessary.

Not every confession in this book is for everyone. On some topics, some of you don't need a confession; you deserve an apology. And so, when you arrive at each confession section, it is my hope you will be able to discern when it's appropriate to receive the confession as opposed to offering it.

Following each confession will always be a declaration of forgiveness. This I offer not with certainty; I'm not convinced I have the power to absolve anyone, especially if I am not the one who's been wounded. But I include these declarations because self-forgiveness can be a deadly serious and necessary thing if we are to survive, if we are to reclaim interior rest. Have you offered apology? Have you made reparation? Are you becoming more human? Forgive yourself.

BENEDICTION—Traditionally spoken over congregations at the end of religious services, benedictions are final words of blessing as we depart from the liturgy. These benedictions can be read like a melding of both letter and prayer. I am praying to you and the divine at once. You might consider it a final declaration of imagination: the humanity I want for us. This is what I dream we carry with us as we close the book.

CONTEMPLATION—What does it mean to stay near to our interior worlds? To travel through those hidden corridors of the heart where we have hesitated to go? As we listen for the stories, emotions, loves, hungers, and dreams that reside in us, we liberate all that the world obscures from us. At the close of each liturgy in Part One, you will find several questions for contemplation. The significance of each question lies not in its answer (there are no right, wrong, or static ones), but in the listening itself—a sacred attention.

LITURGIES FOR OCCASION—The second half of this book is organized by seasons or occasions, some following a Christian calendar. They can be encountered alone but are written with an imagination for being recited in community.

You'll notice that a call-and-response form is used, in accordance with a long line of liturgical rituals that predate us. This form tends to bring out new tensions and release in us. For example, some of us have only known our role as leader; it may be challenging to submit to belonging to the company of responders. Perhaps these liturgies can guide you into a kind of rest. You don't always have to set the tone, to decide, to steer. Or perhaps you have long been silenced or alienated in spiritual spaces. Is this an opportunity for your voice to be centered—not dismissed, but waited on, heeded? I hope. You deserve that much.

Some of the occasions in Part Two will apply to you, and others won't. A number of the liturgies are born of the Catholic Christian story. I name this only to warn that it may at times feel exclusive to a particular kind of reader. I've included a template for writing one's own liturgy at the end of the book, as a very small gesture to those of you who might like to write liturgies that feel closer to the occasions you experience.

Finally, you do not need my permission, but if it helps, this is a reminder that you have agency in how and what you encounter in this book. Pass over what doesn't feel right for you, remain where you need to remain. There is no order. There is no demand I will make of you, apart from staying near to yourself, your body, your own soul, and the stories that dwell there.

Part One
By Story

1

DIGNITY

When God had made [the human], he made him out of stuff that sung all the time and glittered all over. Then after that some angels got jealous and chopped him into millions of pieces, but still he glittered and hummed. So they beat him down to nothing but sparks but each little spark had a shine and a song. So they covered each one over with mud. And the lonesomeness in the sparks make them hunt for one another.

—ZORA NEALE HURSTON

*I am so perfect so divine so ethereal so surreal
I cannot be comprehended
    except by my permission*

—NIKKI GIOVANNI

LETTER I | TO THOSE WITH HEADS BOWED TOO LONG

I'm writing this first letter from bed. I lie here on my left side, peeking my right hand from underneath the empty duvet to type. It is not practical, but it is necessary because I'm in pain again and depressed again, and this is all I have to give today.

I've waited months to begin, far too many to admit to my editor now. I wanted upright Cole to write this book—upright and at the eighteenth-century oak desk I bought to make me feel big, like a real writer. Instead, I write this book of liturgies under sheets stained from last night's pumpkin curry. Beside me is a nightstand covered in medications, half-drank mugs of tea, and a littering of elaborate skincare I haven't touched in weeks. I don't feel very big today.

But just now, the man I try to love creaks the door open—slowly, carefully. He perches at the far end of the bed, without speaking, giving me space to adjust to another person in the room. Then he places a bowl of grapes on top of the duvet and nudges it toward me. I pause, stretch out a twitchy arm, and pop one grape into each side of my mouth, and he scoots closer. A hand to my legs, the legs that have only risen to go to the bathroom and back for a week. Closer. Then, *If you never write another word again*... And instead of finishing he just stares at me. Nods. And I know. On his way out, he takes what mugs he can and closes the door behind him.

I don't know what dignity is. Not cognitively. But I know what it feels like. To be loved, to receive honor, to be encountered as a human, not because of any demonstration or performance of such, but because, in mystery, your very being is a miracle, your existence a delicate stitch in the cosmos. Dignity will never depend on anyone's belief in it, certainly not your own. It is not born of writing, even excellent writing. Or excellent research or beautiful architecture or good parenting. It is inherent. If I never write another word, my dignity cannot be diminished. And yet, the world has a choice: to honor or not to honor. The toll this choice takes has very real implications on our rights, our wealth, our justice, our children, and even our *perceptions* of dignity, but never dignity itself.

If my hands can take it, I'm going to wash my hair today. Wash day is my dignity ritual. It requires precisely the same tenderness and patience the world withholds from Black women. In a world that demeans this body—these hands, this scalp—I, in mysterious paradox, am required to meet them with grave compassion. I let my fingers dance and dip, freeing every tangle. I cradle each tendril like gold as it passes through the Denman brush. What used to feel like a punishment has become an honoring. It is a liturgy of reverence. I don't need the liturgy in order to become dignified, but it reminds me of the miracle, of the inherent beauty of life lived in this body. With these particular hands, with this particular curl pattern. Wash day asks me to look up. To behold.

Our liturgies begin with dignity, because that is where any kind of liberation begins: with an awareness that you are worthy of so much more than whatever form your chains have taken today. For now, you are here—breathing, being, granting a gift that cannot be replicated. Your simple, miraculous, necessary existence.

Believing with you,

C

Terracotta

All the empty
bowls are beginning
to wonder why I keep shattering
them on marble
countertops because
my hands
aren't what they were.

I was still collecting
shards when you called
me to say
there's no such thing
as collapsed lungs
from speaking
too loud. But that you shouldn't
sleep with your chin tucked
into your own chest
and you should never
dream with your mouth open
letting anything make its home in you.
And I remember

Something about the way my father held
the mirror, saying
If it's a storm,
You're the lightning
his sparkling sunken eyes
waiting above
the backwards me.
He lifts my chin up by a string.

All the empty bowls
are beginning
to wonder
why I hold
these hands like a miracle.

Prayers

FOR WORTH

God in us,
We know the miracle inherent in our existence. We are here, our
beauty stretching out and dwelling within us. But it is hard to believe
in one's dignity when the systems and societies to which we belong
are content to destroy us. We have heard lies of our worthlessness in
the explicit and implicit ways the world interacts with our bodies,
stories, and homes. It is incessant—this lie of our own inadequacy,
this charade of our inferiority. Remind us that our dignity does not
wane or bud in relation to anyone's belief in it, including our own.
Let us rest with the knowledge that we have nothing to prove; our
dignity, perpetual as it is divine. We will not shrink. We expand. Remind us of our making. For we too contain the divine. *Amen.*

FOR LITTLE BLACK GIRLS

God of the Black girl,
We call on your protection. Release us from the kind of fear that
doesn't lead to wisdom, and grant us that wisdom which guides our
souls from danger. We pray that when others look on us, they would
be freed from the evil whispers that drive them—the hidden voice
that seeks to discredit and villainize us, claiming we are too callous,
too angry, too dramatic. May our glory confound all those who despise us; let them learn to gaze on it without impulse to devour it.
Guide us to communities that see us in the fullness of our humanity; and regardless of the honor withheld from us by the world, let
us walk in the unwavering knowledge of our dignity. Let us marvel
at the elders and ancestors who walked before us, knowing that our
story is entwined with theirs; that we come from a brilliance of
mind and heart. Free us from the lie that our beauty and brilliance

are things to be proven but let the truth of them hold us like the warmth of the wombs that formed us. *Ase.*

FOR DECOLONIZING YOUR INTERIOR LANDSCAPE

God who reclaims,

One moment we are free, jaws unclenched and at home with ourselves. Then, without warning, a wind passes through us, sending a thousand tiny uncertainties ricocheting through our inner worlds. We question our beauty, our power and memory. We grow suspicious of love and feel foolish for our hope. Remind us that it's not our fault. Let us remember that a society constructed by the oppressor never wanted us free. We've been conditioned toward a very particular form of seeing; we have been indoctrinated into the illusion that says white is pure and black is sinful. That says our worth is correlated with how willing we are to be eaten and spit out by capitalist appetite. That says power is measured by the force with which we take someone else's agency. Travel with us into our interior worlds, reclaiming every site that has been colonized, every location of internalized hatred and dishonor. Take us home to ourselves. And let us remember what it feels like to say our own names with the reverence they demand. Take us home. *Amen.*

FOR THOSE WHO DARE DEGRADE

God who keeps watch,

Woe to those who dare degrade us. May we see them for what they are, and call wicked by its name. Awaken in us a sacred intuition that exposes those who work exhaustively against our welfare. We're tired of protecting them. We're tired of easing them into the realization of their own violence, the ugly that has made its home in them. May they writhe in the night. May their inner worlds tremble. Make the secret guilt that drives them grow loud enough to shame them. Let the sound reach those who need protection, and may we have the wisdom to trust our instincts, believing ourselves when a space or moment doesn't feel safe even if we cannot articulate why. God, keep watch, keep guard, as we wait for the day when the terrible become human again. *May it be so.*

FOR TRANS AND NONBINARY LIVES

God of our truest names,
We confess that too often we have encountered liberation in a person and chosen hatred. We confess our own jealousy at a person capable of living into their true self, when we ourselves are suffocating. We are in bondage to binaries that limit our imaginations for full liberation. Remind us that you yourself contain multitudes. Let us encounter the divine that refuses to be contained by human definition or imagination. Expose all the ways we neglect trans people in our activism. Expose the moral rot that makes us so terrified of publicly supporting Black trans women. Let us become honest about the hatred we have inherited, the violence enacted against queer folk at the hands of those who came before us—Christianity playing no small part in a culture of transphobia. Protect those with the courage to stay near to themselves. May their liberation be multiplied in all who encounter it. *Amen.*

FOR BEING HUMAN

God of shalom,
Here we are dangling one another from the precipice without care or concern for our collective fate. We have lost sight of our own faces, risking our humanity in favor of supremacy. Guide us away from the edge of our undoing. Show us what it means to be people of deep and abiding reverence for the beauty and connectedness of everything everywhere. Train us out of habits of degradation and artifice—incessantly competing to be worth more, to be loved more. Remind us that we don't need to exalt humanity over any other piece of creation in order to be worth something. Keep us from the

delusion of our dominion over earth, sky, or star. We are no greater. Remind us that the dust beneath us transcends our own humble existence, and let our hardened exteriors soften in the presence of safety. May any honor we've withheld from one another be doubled in the presence of reparation and forgiveness. We won't get free alone. Keep us human. *Amen.*

Breathe

In a position of rest, place the palm of your hand to your chest. If it feels safe to do so, close your eyes. Feel where you may be carrying tension in your body. Release what you can.

Silently name and hold the first phrase as you inhale.
Silently name and hold the second phrase as you exhale.
Breathe deeply and slowly to start and adjust to what feels possible and right in your body.
Choose and remain with a breath prayer for as long as you need.

INHALE: We honor this breath.
EXHALE: We behold the beauty.

INHALE: I deserve more.
EXHALE: I claim more.

INHALE: This flesh is sacred.
EXHALE: I contain the divine.

Confession

Creator God,
We confess every attempt to steal and grant dignity, as if it's something we have dominion over. We have lost ourselves in a world of anti-Blackness, transphobia, homophobia, ableism, and misogyny. We have amplified the cool and the confident and alienated those

who feel strange or awkward. In demeaning others, we mistakenly believe that our own self-worth may be magnified, but in doing so we only become less human. We have not become bigger but smaller. Not safer but more afraid. Every effort to diminish the worth of another has only distanced us from the truth of our own dignity. Forgive us. And remind us of who we are, what we're made of, that a collective image of God is dwelling in and through us. May we forgive ourselves and become faithful keepers of our cosmic birthright to beauty, justice, and belonging. *Amen.*

Forgiveness

Let your soul receive this rest: The God who became seamstress, the God who knelt in the garden to make clothes for Eve and Adam, covers you now. As the divine meets your shame with tenderness, you are freed to stand before the earth, neighbor, your God, and yourself. *Amen.*

Benediction

May the God who made all things and holds together all things remind you of your making. May you rest in the immanence of your own worth, knowing you have nothing to prove and everything to love. Constant as the moon, which is tethered to us by unseen forces, which is suspended above us in the dark and the light, let our dignity remain, be it visible or invisible to those below. And may we remember, the same dignity that holds us, so too holds together every person and piece of the cosmos at once and evermore. Go, in honor, to claim all that you are worthy of. *May it be so.*

Contemplation

1. Choose a posture or small practice you can adopt to ground yourself in your worth daily. When will you practice this? How will it connect you to the glory of your body?

2. Explore a memory of when you felt unworthy or demeaned in childhood. What do you wish you could say to yourself, or someone else, that you didn't believe then?

3. Who is someone who has affirmed your dignity in a meaningful way? How did that affirmation come—words, humor, attention, justice?

4. What is the relationship between art and dignity? What art is helping you to heal your self-belief in this season?

5. Reflect on a moment when you wanted someone else to feel small. Toni Morrison said, "If you can only be tall because somebody's on their knees, then you have a serious problem." What is the origin of that problem for you? How did you receive the message that dignity is a scarcity—something to be won at someone else's expense?

2

SELFHOOD

I feel lonely and serious. Something has been happening to me, a change that has been a long time coming. I want to be real. —ASSATA SHAKUR

I could no more escape than I could think of my identity. Perhaps, I thought, the two things are involved with each other. When I discover who I am, I'll be free.

—RALPH ELLISON

LETTER II | TO THOSE WHOSE NAME GETS CAUGHT IN THEIR THROAT

If you don't know, my first name is actually Nicole. My name was supposed to be Breonna, but after the C-section, while my mom was asleep, my dad went rogue and began telling everyone, including the nurses, that my name was Nicole. Until my mom finally woke up and said, *Who the hell is Nicole?* And maybe she was too tired to argue, because Breonna was buried, and Nicole remained.

In childhood, despite my resistance, I was given the nickname Nikki. Nikki felt like it belonged to someone happy, perky even. I did not know her. But I was too timid to assert myself with regularity, so it slowly became the default among some family members. Nikki eventually became Nick, which I feel neutral about. Then Nickabock, which was a tragedy.

It wasn't until college that I remembered another name. My little brother, side by side with my ten-year-old self as we rocked and swayed on a rusting playset out back, named me by accident. *Cole* slid from his mouth with an urgency, skipping over the *Ni*. He didn't correct himself; he just laughed and pumped his legs out once more and said, *Be a boy so I can call you that.* And what I didn't say then, but realized years later and miles away from him, was that I was home in that moment, flying on that rusting swing set with him, letting our bodies flail and push and do what they had to without anyone else's gaze stuck to us. His was an honest mistake, but not every truth is found on purpose. And so I became Cole. Not by everyone immediately; I was far too distant from my own voice back then. But by college, I was ready. I knew my name.

Years later, on my wedding day, all of these names converged. The priest calls me Cole, and it's grave, serious—me, as I've known myself. My father strokes my face and whispers, *Nicole, babygirl.* My uncle jukes toward me before drawing me in, *What's good, Nick Nick?* Even Nikki made her appearance, and for once this felt right, too; I could access the joy in it that day. And these people, who all their lives had known a variation of me, collided. I was terrified for this collision; I really was. I wasn't nervous to get married, I was worried about having so many sounds of me clanging around at once. Which is to say, I was afraid of myself. Before the ceremony, I peeked through the window. Who would I be? What would my laugh sound like? Am I funny or smart? Am I quiet or charming? What music do I like? How do I dance? Who will I be? And will these people accept this being?

The collision did not end in destruction but union. I floated bravely in and out of different parts of me—sister, niece, daughter, friend, quirky, serious, quiet, rowdy. I will not pretend that fragments of false selves did not likewise appear, but if they did it was immemorable. I couldn't have known it before this day, but somewhere along the way I had found a tether. Something to bind me to who I am when everything goes quiet at night. I know who I am. And it's not necessarily static, but it's consistent in its truth. I'm convinced that most of the time you spend "finding yourself" is really just the practice of admitting who you already know yourself to be in the deepest parts of you.

In his commencement address at Spelman College, Howard Thurman said:

There is something in every one of you that waits, listens for the sound of the genuine in yourself—and if you cannot hear it, you will never find whatever it is for which you are searching and if you hear it and then do not follow it, it was better that you had never been born.... And if you cannot hear the sound of the genuine in you, you will all of your life spend your days on the ends of strings that somebody else pulls.

I know who I am. The sound is unmistakable. The question is, Am I safe enough, am I well enough, am I loved enough to be able to admit it?

I don't know who you are yet, but I believe you do. Who are you when it all goes quiet at night? Who are you by daybreak? What are your loves? Who do you come from? Trace the lines on your hands. What stories are etched there? Can you be still long enough to listen for something true when the noise of the world seeks to muffle the sound of your interior world?

To be people with any concern for the dignity and liberation of everything, we must become unequivocally familiar with our own faces. We must confront those things we've learned to use to obscure our own image. And in divine integrity, we must stay near to ourselves.

I need you whole. Tell me what your name is. I'll cradle every syllable as we swing through rust for the clouds.

Listening with you,

C

running home

no one told me who I was supposed to be that year for halloween and so when I went as a ballerina and you all went as power rangers I tried to make a mask out of my soft pink tutu but only ended up smothering myself and getting laughed at and I know you understand how it feels to be clinging to your face all night wearing someone else's pants but back then you just walked faster and I watched you from behind and tried to imagine your front was mine and your long strides were mine and it was my fist knocking at the stranger's door until I pass myself in a window and remember I'm the one wrapped in lace and I'm the soft one and I'm the silence and I'm the concrete and I'm these legs running and I'm these lungs breathing and I'm a door opening

Prayers

FOR THE JOURNEY BACK TO YOURSELF

Steady God,
We are shape-shifters, drifting in and out of our counterfeit selves depending on whom we are in proximity to. There are days when who we are feels so imprecise, so transient, that we wonder if anything of us is real at all. Turn us toward the parts of us that are true and reveal the parts that are more mask than flesh. Keep us from demonizing our false selves, but let us turn to them in curiosity and compassion; knowing every mask is born of a wound. Travel with us into memories of all that has formed us, those secret places in ourselves where we have hesitated to go. And on the journey, may we listen for the sound of our own name. May we speak it with the conviction of one who knows it by heart. *Amen.*

FOR BEING MORE THAN ONE THING

Fluid God,
Fear can make us demand definition from mystery. We tell stories about your static nature to make the divine digestible to us. We condense and simplify our own stories to make them clear and resolved. Since we were little, we've been dissected not with nuance and complexity, but by a zeitgeist that favors categories and binaries. It feels like we must choose—to be smart or pretty, to be angry or kind, to be masculine or feminine, to be well or wounded. Free us from this confinement. Help us to remember we are not singular, that we are free to be more than one thing. Protect us from a world intent on narrowing our selfhoods. Remind us that these binaries exist not so that we might be understood but so that we might be made small. Guide us as we honor the sacred spectrums within each of us, and within one another. There is a multitude in us. We will not be reduced. *Ase.*

FOR THE ONES WHO ARE HIDING TO SURVIVE

God of the shadows,
We long to be seen, and we're terrified to be seen. We find ourselves in rooms where, to belong, we must disguise and diminish ourselves, our bodies, and our thoughts. Help us to reclaim the sound of our truest voice, learning to name our desires, our loves, our doubts without apology. We can only pretend for so long. May we prioritize our own protection in relationships that demand a particular way of being or thinking or believing. Grant us communities who honor our thoughts, needs, and emotions, and liberate others to do likewise. But until we're safe, until we can come out of hiding without being destroyed, grant us an interior stability. That we would be grounded in who we are, even when the world is not human enough to honor it. Wait with us for the day. *May it be so.*

FOR THOSE WHO'VE CHANGED

God of change,
We are not who we once were. We are tired of being known only in memory. Protect us from being dragged into a selfhood that no longer feels true for us. Help us to walk in our present selves without forgetting or dismissing who we've been—the pain we may have caused, the stories we carry. Remind us that our journey to selfhood is not escapism but listening, attunement. And as we look toward deeper change still, help us to remember that we can honor our future selves without degrading who we have been. There is beauty here too, on the edge of our becoming. *Amen.*

FOR HOLY ARROGANCE

God who expands,
Is there room for us? We've been taught for so long by the white-supremacist capitalist patriarchy to trivialize our strengths, lessen our intellect. We've been told that we are only beautiful if we play

small. But we are proud of ourselves, God. And our beauty is not discreet. Exorcise the lie that naming our worth could somehow compromise it. Grant us a holy audacity to be precisely who we are, taking up the space that we need to breathe freely. Keep us from choosing self-deprecation for the sake of someone else's comfort. We will not shrink. God, let us expand. *Amen.*

FOR WHEN YOU'RE MISUNDERSTOOD

Divine Labyrinth,
Who can truly understand us? Most days, we confuse even ourselves. We say what we don't want to say. We choose what we don't wish to keep. So often, it feels like our words, our actions, are only guiding people away from what is really true of us. We are lost to one another. Grasping for a hand like children in the dark. We want to be found and we're terrified to be found. Here in the center of the maze of us, God, it's lonely. Help us to call out to one another. Grant us endurance and patience as we locate one another through miscommunication, through charade, through grief, through anger. Make us tender observers of the unseen, the unspoken; and keep us on the path, until we at last meet face-to-face. *Amen.*

Breathe

INHALE: I know who I am.
EXHALE: I am near to myself.

INHALE: I am still being made.
EXHALE: I can honor my becoming.

INHALE: I will listen for my voice.
EXHALE: I come home to myself.

Confession

God aware,

We confess all of the ways we have participated in our own vanishing. We are desperate for a place to hide, even from ourselves. We confess that we have wanted to disappear, sometimes out of self-hatred, but also out of the incessant terrors of this world. We have fled from our own interior worlds, afraid of what we might suffer if we become honest. We have resented our own faces, our mannerisms, our desires, and instead have chosen a mask. We believed this mask to be necessary for our survival. But we know now, it was erasure. Rescue us from those illusions that are not for our protection, and forgive us for all the ways we demand that others hide or mask in our presence. Have mercy on us, that we may stay near to our own souls. *Amen.*

Forgiveness

Let your soul receive this rest: Take heart. You, who are fighting the current of self-neglect and self-loathing, are doing the best you can. As the forgiveness of God comes awake in you, may you have mercy on the complexities of your own interior world and liberate it daily. You don't have to run from yourself. Take your time. *Amen.*

Benediction

Now may the sound of the genuine in you stir anew, that you would stay near enough to yourself to decipher the truth of who you are—what you crave, how you communicate, how you love, what you're afraid of—and when it's safe and right, choose to unmask. As you rise to meet your own face, may you be at rest. *May it be so.*

Contemplation

1. What do you think makes up one's selfhood? How much is a result of what has happened to us, and how much do you believe is inherent? Does it matter to you that the two be distinguishable?
2. We often spend a great deal of energy trying to manufacture a singular, static self. Try a small practice of daily attunement. Pause, breathe. What is true of you today? What do you hear when you listen?
3. Travel into a memory when someone else's articulation of you felt in conflict with who you knew yourself to be. How did you align with or resist their determination of you? What did they get wrong? What was the toll in being misunderstood?
4. Where do you feel most at home with yourself? What sensations do you feel in your body as you imagine yourself there?

3

PLACE

Like the dead-seeming, cold rocks, I have memories within that came out of the material that went to make me. Time and place have had their say.

—ZORA NEALE HURSTON

I believe that one can never leave home. I believe that one carries the shadows, the dreams, the fears and dragons of home under one's skin, at the extreme corners of one's eyes and possibly in the gristle of the earlobe.

—MAYA ANGELOU

LETTER III | TO WHEREVER YOU ARE

As I write these letters, I've often found myself imagining *where* you are. I've pictured your hands holding the pages, your faces even. I've wondered where you sit or lie; if the chair beneath you is soft or hard; what the weather is doing outside your windows. Wherever you are, I hope you are safe.

This is what you should know about my home.

It's old. Its age—183 years—makes it both lovely and daunting. The red bricks have limed to a pinkish hue, and a dark green ivy is draped over its side. It's tall and romantic and you should know this. But time has had its say, tucking secrets in every corner. The glass panes rattle in the wind, and the floor planks whine even on tiptoes.

In the basement, there's a room filled with rubble. The room has no door, so as you pass by it to get to the sump pump, you are witness to the dusty chunks of stone resting shin-deep in the dark. On the day of the home inspection, I saw it. But to everyone else it seemed no greater deal than the wall color in the bathroom or the shape of the kitchen counters, so I didn't ask. I just stood there silently, stealing glances at the broken stone piled through the doorway, as men in boots explained to me what a sump pump was. You may find my silence strange, but the house is very old, and I am very socially anxious. I assumed my husband understood what and why it was. Until one evening, just a year after we moved in, he looked up from his bowl of zuppa toscana and asked, simply and suddenly, *What do you think is with that room of rubble?*

I wonder sometimes what is hidden underneath. What is lost in the deep gaps of those stones. Snakes . . . mice . . . bones? The possibilities are unsettling. *Is the house crumbling? What about radon?* There have been nights when I lie in bed awake haunted by the thought of what the rubble means for us. But most days, I try to pretend it's not there at all. And can I tell you something? The basement is a mirror. It is a portal to the things in me that I'd prefer remain hidden. It is not metaphor, not quite. It is real and it's dark and its dust makes your eyes sting. But how I confront the rubble reveals to me how I confront the hiddenness of other things.

So much of our formation rests on our relationship to place. Is your home a site of terrors—ankles folding in half, necks coiled into shoulders as you walk across the rubble room? Is it a site of peace—the reliable and gentle clicking of the baseboard heaters in the dead of winter? For many of us, the answer does not belong to this binary. It is less a question of whether our place is good or not, and far more a question of what of it is living in you. And perhaps, what of it is no longer welcome. Some of us were formed in resistance to the ideals of a place, not in loyalty to them. But even then, there are threads in you that can be traced back to the places where you've spent so much time. Maybe this is why nostalgia can feel so solemn; it always contains some form of grief. Grief at what no longer is. Grief at what was never there at all.

What does place have to do with our becoming? Just as I am being formed by the rubble below, so too am I formed by the rooms I've dwelled in before it. By my grandmother's kitchen. The spice mixture in that old tin can, paper bags strewn on countertops as we watch the chicken come out of the oil and find its resting place. I am formed by the boulevard—the one place I ever walked with my chin up because my father told me to walk like I had some sense, and it felt like I finally had a right to be someplace. And now, this old brick house has gotten into me; the crumbling mortar reminding me what trust is. The ivy on the brick makes me feel like I'm not a burden. The heavy tombstone of a door makes me feel safe enough to exhale. And I will tell you the secret of knowing yourself. It will not be found by perpetual disassociation. Look down—this sidewalk, that creaky floorboard, the smell of Saturday—the thing that made you. This beautiful, terrible thing. I'll take it, bones and all.

From below,

C

Milan Avenue

We pronounced you
All wrong.
My as in something that can be possessed.
Lan that sounds
like land.

Your door was lightweight,
Anything but
Sturdy under the palm.
But I could smell you by heart.
Sweet cigar and spearmint,
Metallic fingertips after turning
A knob, tarnished.

When we'd sit in your empty
Tub, pretending to be soldiers.
The plastic curtain
We said was skin—
Its speckled vinyl clinging to us with wet
From someone else's shower.

Your floors squealed with us.
Your brick crumbled with us.

Italy will never know you
Like we do.
Magic,
Dreadful and ours,
Dangling from every shingle.

Prayers

FOR THE WALK HOME

God of the street you know by heart,
I know these steps. They're etched with memories, reminding me I
am made of story. As I pass each building, each door, travel with me
into my former selves. Keep me from that nostalgia which chains
me to the past, but help me smell and taste and listen and feel and
observe all that has made me. Help me become curious how my
sense of home is responsible for my formation. But may I do so with
self-compassion, never daring to travel streets my inner child is unsafe or unprepared to encounter. As I turn corners and peek down
alleys, as I speed up and slow down, may I at last make my way
home. And if that home be entirely new—safer, kinder, truer—
may my inmost being find the rest and comfort I was made for.
Amen.

FOR LEAVING

God who left,
We have known what it means to feel alone in a crowded room. For
too long have we sacrificed our selfhood to achieve a kind of belonging. We have been held captive by communities more interested in
controlling us than loving us. Remind us that just because a place is
deeply known by us does not mean it is safe. Protect us from any
guilt we feel for leaving. Expose every unhealthy attachment, as we
move toward bonds that honor who we are today. It is hard, God, to
believe that you might be preparing a kinder and more loving place
for us. Grant us imagination for a promised land as we step out into
the wilderness. *Amen.*

FOR THOSE WHOSE HOMES WERE, OR ARE, UNSAFE

God of locked doors,
Some of us are haunted. Home has not been a place of rest for us. Our shoulders stiffen, our bellies ache, our heads throb with the anxiety of never knowing if the threat is awake or asleep. Remind us that we were never meant to know what our chests feel like when that doorknob turns or this floorboard creaks. This haunting, help us to escape. Accompany us toward the door as we honor the cost of displacement, while believing that we are worthy of peace. Let our boundaries be honored, that we would not be guilted or gaslit back through the threshold of chaos. Help us to be patient with ourselves as we find safer spaces, granting us discernment to distinguish the real from the illusory. As we search for a place of true rest, may we find home in the liminal, in the unknown or in-between. And even, home in ourselves. *Amen.*

FOR THE PLACES THAT WERE STOLEN FROM US

God who reclaims,
Some of us didn't choose to leave. Whether by abduction or invasion, our place was stolen from us. When the colonizer is so miserable with their own life, when they hate themselves enough so acutely, they flee their home to consume someone else's. Reveal how that same self-hatred and hunger are still awake in many today. Expose them, God, that we would recognize wolves when they arrive at our doorstep. That their occupation of, and reign over, lands that were never theirs would come to an end. There are those of us whose connection to our native land was stolen so long ago that we have never fully grieved it. Allow us to explore our loss, that we would not be rushed to accept the way things are. Ground all who are displaced in a sense of self and home. Show us that we are, at all times, tethered to the ancestors who remember all that we cannot. *Ase.*

FOR THE KITCHEN

God of the kitchen table,
We are grateful for the mysteries of our mother's kitchen, our grand-mother's frying pan, our father's spices. May our kitchens belong to a legacy of resistance and reclamation. In a world where we have not always been granted agency, may we choose and experiment. Under a patriarchy that does not trust Black women, may we trust ourselves, eyeing every seasoning, feeling the recipe not as command but as soul. Remind us that this is a site of innovation, at times making miracles out of what little we've had, our hands multiplying food in divine mystery. Protect the kitchen conversations—the laughter, the community organizing, the remembrance that are so often practiced at the table or counters, as we wait for food that will remind us what we're worthy of. And as we think back on all that has formed us throughout time, may we remember that what happens here is sacred—that we made a space for us. May we eat and be filled. *Ase.*

FOR THE LAND

God of creature and sky,
We have not protected the divine in all of creation. We have forgot-ten our origins, placing ourselves as superior to the very earth that formed us. Humble us, God; shake us from the belief that we are capable of ruling over the earth when we cannot even care for hu-manity. Remind us just how young we are in comparison to the cosmos. We are no saviors; make us learners. Make us listen for and heed the quiet things whispered by the soil and sea. Free us from our narcissism as we look on the suffering of other creatures and find our souls at last stirred. And as we become honest about our flagrant degradation of land, may we protect those countries and peoples who have disproportionately suffered the greed of the pow-erful. May we listen to the Indigenous wisdom in our midst, those who have long warned us that this land does not belong to us—that our ownership of it is our collective delusion. As we look up from

the lie, may we find tree and star and dirt, and become the earth's meekest disciples and fiercest protectors. *Amen.*

Breathe

INHALE: I know this place.
EXHALE: This is holy ground.

INHALE: I am rooted.
EXHALE: I am home.

INHALE: Take me where it's safe.
EXHALE: God, prepare a place.

Confession

God our home,
We are lost. We have mistaken an untethered life for an awakened one. We roam from place to place at great cost to the earth beneath us, believing that we will *find* ourselves. We have stolen the homes of others because we cannot bear to gaze upon our own scorched earth. We have made a performance out of pretending like we are not a product of where we once called home. We have failed to contend with how our own actions render a space more or less welcoming or safe. Forgive us our escapism and neglect, and in your mercy let us encounter the places we come from without turning against ourselves. *Amen.*

Forgiveness

Let your soul receive this rest: The God who made dirt and sky, stone and sand, is present with us wherever we find ourselves. Believe the divine can restore our relationships to place, that we would be free to leave and free to remain, not out of fear or greed but out of an understanding for all that forms us. *Amen.*

Benediction

May God our home forgive our appetite for spaces that don't belong to us. May they have mercy on the colonized and the abducted, the refugee and the immigrant, and take us where it's safe and honoring. In time may you be liberated out of exile and wilderness and delivered back home to yourself. *Amen.*

Contemplation

1. When you think of home, what do you feel and where do you feel it in your body?
2. Are you more prone to nomadism or rootedness? What desires led to this? What fears?
3. What sensory-based memories do you have of your childhood home? Describe the smells. What noises did your home make? How did the carpet feel underfoot?
4. How has your community influenced you? What of your values were formed because of, or in spite of, the environments to which you've belonged?
5. How have displacement and dislocation presented in your life?
6. Reflect on your interior landscape. Which places in yourself do you travel into when your physical setting feels unsafe or distant?

4

WONDER

The world is full of painful stories. Sometimes it seems as though there aren't any other kind and yet I found myself thinking how beautiful that glint of water was through the trees. —OCTAVIA BUTLER

They shared an unshakeable belief in beauty, in overflow, in everythingness, the bursting, indelible beauty in a world where there is so much suffering and wounding and pain. —ELIZABETH ALEXANDER

LETTER IV | TO THOSE AT REST ON PARK BENCHES

I drove to the lake to write this letter. Perhaps I thought it would move me, looking out into the distance. But my eyes are bothering me today so I can't stare at the lake. It's too bright toward the sun.

But to my left, there's an old man trying to fly a kite with a child. I've decided it's his grandson. I pivot my body just so to watch them twist and tug at the string. The purple nylon octopus stares up at me with mouth agape, as it thrashes and flaps against the grass. And the little old man is saying, *Take it and run, take it and run.* And the boy does, only there always seems to be a pause between the passing of the string and that first step. So the kite drifts up for a moment, then crashes back to the ground. And maybe on another day this would be a tragedy, but the man and child are laughing hard enough for all of us. The man begins grabbing the octopus by the mouth and shooting it like a dart toward the sky. *Now run, go!* And the boy just rocks back on his heels and laughs.

You might wonder if they ever got it in the air, if the octopus took flight and soared above as we marveled and clapped. That is not this story, and it never met the sky. Not this day. But now, they're sitting on the bench next to mine sharing orange slices. Have you ever been doing something and suddenly you realize you're smiling? Like your whole face is playing a trick on you? Well, I'm grinning now as I watch sideways from my bench. They're squirting juice from the oranges at each other. The boy licks it up off his hand and puts it out for a handshake. The man nods and solemnly obliges. A small head tucks into his sticky arms.

There are days when the sun is too bright, when the majestic feels like the kind of beautiful you cannot approach. Look to your left. The beauty you seek can be found in the mundane. A man holding a boy holding a worn nylon octopus, and maybe you're grinning too.

In a time when we have more access than ever before to the traumas of this world, how will you resist the tide of despair? Let beauty be your anchor. If you find the lake view too bright, bring your gaze closer, perhaps all the way to your own flesh and blood. Life is monstrous on the threshold of apocalypse. The practice of beholding, this fidelity to beauty in all things, I've come to believe, is no small form of salvation.

In awe,

C

Chronicle

How the moon rests on the tip of Gulf Tower like it's touched
Down to earth to visit for a while.
How the small man at the bus stop folds his arms and closes his
eyes knowing
He has enough time.
How the faces carved in stone hover above people
Asleep on the cathedral steps.
How headlights live in puddles on nights when
The city becomes its own mirror.
How remnants of rain creep down the window after
The sky has cleared.
How you forget how to breathe the moment
You remember you are.
How you look at me and I don't
Look away.

All beauty occurring
Twice, being
Seen and unseen.

Prayers

FOR BEAUTY IN THE MUNDANE

God of every beautiful thing,
Make us people of wonder. Show us how to hold on to nuance and
vision when our souls become addicted to pain, to the unlovely. It is
far easier to see the gloom and decay; so often it sings a louder song.
Attune our hearts to the good still stirring in our midst, not that we
would give ourselves to toxic positivity or neglect the pain of the
world, but that we would be people capable of existing in the tension. Grant us habits of sacred pause. Let us marvel not just at the
grand or majestic, but beauty's name etched into every ordinary
moment. Let the mundane swell with a mystery that makes us
breathe deeper still. And by this, may we be sustained and kept
from despair. *Amen.*

FOR WHAT YOU FIND ON THE MOUNTAINTOP

God above,
We thank you for allowing us to journey up. That we would be able
to see a place not just from within it but from a distance is a gift we
do not readily comprehend. Here, as we look out at what seems as
if it can fit in the palm of our hand, remind us of beauty's vastness.
In this moment may we be both large and small. Remind us that
beauty isn't merely for our consumption, but that it is something to
be protected. Grow in us a wonder that is willing to bow to the
beauty of the natural world, that it would be a path to humility and
not ego. That we would understand it does not exist *for* us, but it is
our divine fortune that we would be moved by it. And we are moved,
God. May this view form us and keep us, as we allow our souls to
remain stirred when we return to the ground we've known. *May it
be so.*

FOR WHAT HAPPENS INSIDE YOU AS YOU STARE OUT AT BODIES OF WATER

God of inner calm,
Something about the water leads us into ourselves. As we gaze out at the sky dancing on the soft, fluid surface, we are steadied. Let this moment be an entrance to new ways of knowing the self, the world, and the God that sent them. May the waters that sway remind us that there is rhythm to the advents and departures of this world. That what is lost will be found again—never precisely the same water, but found nonetheless like the promise of the tide returning. Grant us wisdom and stability of heart to discern when the waves are safe and when they mean to destroy us. May the waters that run be a mystical assurance that there are some things that we can depend on. The river flows downhill; let the certainty of that relieve the anxiety of all that remains unknown. Help us to marvel at its sound as it carves time's impression into the land that surrounds it. And may still waters guide us into safe introspection, their mirrored face showing us our own faces with stunning clarity, teaching us what it means to rest without apology. God of the depths and shallows, *hear our prayer.*

FOR THE SKYLINE

Divine Architect,
It is far easier to marvel at the landscape of the field or forest than the streets and neighborhoods that surround us daily. The familiar is the most necessary but most neglected of beauties. Train us to behold what structures and buildings we pass each day. Allow us to marvel at the miracles of our own hands; that the human imagination has dreamt a way out of stone, wood, glass, and brick. We have carved faces into ornamented crown molding. We have hand-hewed wood for beam and table. We have cut stone and melted sand and painted with gold. Remind us that beauty can collide with service, not that we would reduce art's value to its utility, but that we could

celebrate when it provides shelter to those who behold it. As we stare out at the skyline, draw our eyes to materials, to shapes, to reflections, and so too draw our eyes toward the meek and the simple of our own neighborhoods. The buildings that remain even in our neglect of them—a sacred defiance in a world that has not cared well for those who dwell there. May we marvel at that which has endured decay and abandonment and stands, however solid or frail, in resistance. *Amen.*

FOR MARVELING AT YOUR OWN FACE

God of the flesh,

When we consider what is worthy of our wonder, it is easy to forget our own faces, our bodies. The world is relentless in indoctrinating us into self-hatred—into anti-Blackness, into transphobia, into misogyny in all forms. We are slowly and steadily brainwashed to despise our own faces from the time we're tall enough to stare up at ourselves in the mirror. How can we resist this? Let the tyranny of the mirror be no more. May it instead become a portal—to delight, to pleasure, and to love. These noses, these hips, the way our hair rises and falls. The memories etched into our hands and faces. Remind us of the miracle of flesh that grows back, of blood that pulses warm beneath the skin that holds us. Of bodies, these holy beautiful bodies, that are working a thousand unseen miracles just so that we can read these lines, breathe this air, cry or not cry. As we peer into the face before us, remind us that we are something to behold. We believe; forgive our unbelief. *Ase.*

FOR STARGAZING

God of sacred darkness,

When the sun sets and the night stretches before us, we are so quick to turn on the light—some of us stricken by fear and anxiety, some by restlessness. We are unwilling to slow down, the way our bodies are meant to do in the dark. Remind us to look up. As we retreat from the bright artificial lights of our days, make us grateful for the sky's sacred dark, which suspends the stars above us. That light is made lovely by blackness reminds us of the beauty of tension and harmony. And may we remember our own smallness and relationship to this glory; that we are one small and necessary fragment in a cosmic community. No greater or less than the sky that covers us or the beetle underfoot. May this beauty secure us in our creational belonging and steady us in divine company. *Ase.*

Breathe

INHALE: God, awaken my soul to beauty.
EXHALE: I resist the tyranny of despair.

INHALE: I can pause to behold.
EXHALE: I am healed in beauty's wake.

INHALE: I choose a life enchanted.
EXHALE: There is miracle in the mundane.

Confession

God of delight,
We confess that we have grown numb to the beauty of this world. We have not protected what is good and true and enchanting. We have forgotten how to marvel at the mundane with the same gravity as we would behold the mountain or valley. We have not looked up to witness the miracle of our architecture. And in our self-hatred, we have failed to delight in and honor the faces we pass each day, including our own. Forgive us our inattention, and in your mercy remind us that we are so much more than our pain. Guide our gaze toward the beautiful. *Amen.*

Forgiveness

Let your soul receive this rest: The same God who makes the death of the tree burst with color can draw us into wonder even in the midst of tragedy. May the divine have mercy on our inattention, that we could grieve what should not be and delight in all that survives us. *Amen.*

Benediction

So may you fall in love again and again with the beautiful. And may that enchantment keep you from the captivity of despair and usher you into dreaming. In your beholding, may you become a faithful protector of every person and piece of creation, including the earth that trembles beneath your feet. Go in peace, to pay attention. *May it be so.*

Contemplation

1. When are you most inclined to practice wonder? What form of art or nature tends to stir your soul?
2. When was the last time beauty disrupted you? Did you resent its disruption or welcome it?
3. Is wonder a privilege? Is it possible to lack access to beauty?
4. Who in your life is an audience of beauty? What of them have you suppressed in yourself and how?
5. Are you more inclined to marvel at nature or human artistry? Why do you think this is?
6. Travel into a memory of when something mundane captivated you. What allowed you to be attentive to beauty in that moment?

5

ARTISTRY

All art is a kind of confession, more or less oblique. All artists, if they are to survive, are forced, at last, to tell the whole story, to vomit the anguish up.
—JAMES BALDWIN

The artist's role is to raise the consciousness of the people. To make them understand life, the world and themselves more completely. That's how I see it. Otherwise, I don't know why you do it. —AMIRI BARAKA

LETTER V | TO THOSE BRAVE ENOUGH TO MAKE

Have I told you that my grandmother was a writer? Her artistry was both purposeful and accidental, like how your breathing deepens when you sit in the right position. It wasn't so much a choice as it was a posture. My whole life I watched strings of words slide out of her like poetry. Sparse and intentional, every pause silencing the room and leaving us to piece ourselves back together (as one often does in the presence of stark beauty). Standing over my bloodied knees, she told me, *No one dies tonight, only petals fall till dawn.* Watching me waiting for the phone to ring, she told me, *Don't let that girl be your air.* After, she'd just move on with a shrug as if she didn't notice she had just sent me home to myself. I think about this. Does the poet necessarily apprehend her power? How much of one's artistry depends on one's belief in it?

Nine months ago, my first book was published. Because of the pandemic and my body, my first in-person lecture was just last week. I spoke at this small liberal arts college in Massachusetts, and afterward an older woman with graying hair and a slowness in her walk came over to me with the book pressed against her chest. She stretched it out to me and instead of the book, I found our hands tangled up in each other. We didn't let go. She looked me in the eyes, and it felt like looking away would have been a kind of betrayal. So we just stood there swaying and trying not to notice when the book slipped in between us and fell to the table. I won't say precisely what words were spoken, but I will tell you that this woman—at least forty years my senior, wisdom hanging from her like skin—told me that my writing had changed her life. Now, I could tell you I felt honored (as I told her, through a grimaced smile), but it was dread I felt. A nagging, desperate dread.

The same dread rushed toward me on and off all night, like a tide that leaves you a little farther sunken with each departure. Perhaps it was that I thought this woman deserved something greater than my words to affect her. Like my language could never rise to meet the dignity of her. Perhaps it was, as a therapist might suggest, the enduring anxiety of being seen by another, and in some manner encountering myself. Or maybe it was that for all the letters saying that my writing had changed someone, for all the teary-eyed handshakes and pregnant nods, my words that had moved others still hadn't managed to move me.

Our survival as artists—as people—depends on our ability to let our own art move us. To believe in beauty without discrimination, even if that beauty is born of you. My gramma was never able to publish a book. She had a lone poem published in an anthology that I sleep next to like its own altar. But because of her particular place in history, the world denied her artistry far more than it affirmed it. When she told the woman at school that she wanted to be a writer, the woman grinned and suggested she consider teaching kindergarten. The world of publishing was always opaque to her, and entirely disinterested in opening the door. She knew her work mattered to her, but she sparsely believed that her work could ever matter to another. And so I ask myself, What interior stability did it take for my gramma to continue picking up the pen after all those years absent of assurance? How does one retain a fidelity to the art when the world makes no vows to you in return? I think she knew what all enduring artists have known: that the artist's sense of responsibility outweighs their insecurity. And the beauty of the art transcends anyone's recognition of it.

Of all the ways we've learned to occupy ourselves, art requires a distinct mystical courage. A sacred arrogance that says not only do I have a right to be here, but I believe my existence will add to the fabric of the universe. I will make. I will craft into existence. This is unbridled power. Undeterred agency in a world that suppresses ours.

My gramma's art survived by her own belief and despite her own disbelief. When I told her that the poem in the anthology changed me, she smirked softly, dipped her head, and said, *It changed me first.* Whatever audacity my gramma's artistry possessed, I hope someday it is found in me. In you. That you and I would allow the artist in us to come awake; that she would not have to tiptoe nightly through our disbelief. The creative dwells in you; I only hope it is given enough voice to cause disruption. This sacred arrogance is a revolution in its own right.

Creating with you,

C

Bill Withers

In a burnt orange turtleneck waits
until after the last
note to open his eyes.

Old Grey Whistle Test
1972—
Sweat dripping down like
His afro is raining.
Eyes closed,
He's lost but not in himself;
In what came
From him.
I know I know I know I know I know I know
That his making is making him.

Eyes closed waiting to be born—
the sound, contracting,
a map, unfolding.

Prayers

FOR BELIEVING IN YOUR ART WHEN NO ONE ELSE DOES

God of the artist,
Is this worth anything at all? To believe in my art feels impossible
when my work has been rejected, dismissed, used, and discarded for
so long. My ability to view the work for what it is, is fading. Can I
be trusted to judge? Can anyone? Assure me in my calling as an artist, that I would not turn away from myself out of insecurity or
hopelessness. Grant me a sacred arrogance. Train me to marvel at
my artistry with the same gravity that a stranger would. Help me
to take myself seriously again—not that I would avoid the difficult
task of honing my craft but that I would believe in my art enough
to ask a deeper truth of it. And when belief wanes, remind me that
I am enough on my own—and when the art isn't worthy, I still am.
Amen.

FOR WHEN YOU'RE TOO EXHAUSTED TO CREATE

God of renewal,
We have been emptied. We remember what it felt like to have an
intent so awake in us that we could not help but send it to page, to
stanza, to score, or to canvas. We were dreamers once. But we have
given far too much and forgotten to sustain our dreaming. Grant us
rest, that our creative spark might be revived. And grant us humility, that we would understand it is not the responsibility of the
spark to light the whole sky. Allow our art to be both simple and
grand, useful and useless, that we would come unfastened from the
weight of our own expectations. Remind us of what good art, art
born from rested souls, can do in the world. Make our art tell the
truth in strange places. *Amen.*

FOR LETTING GO OF THE WORK

God of the art that will never be seen,
There is art that we offer up to the world and there is art that exists
only for itself. Let us be okay with this. Help us to remember the
beauty of those things we've created that no one will ever gaze
upon, that no one will ever hear or study or speak about. Remind us
that there is value in creating even when it won't be consumed by
another. May we reclaim a kind of private artistry. Let all of these
projects come awake in their sacred hiddenness; may they find some
manner of liberation by virtue of their secrecy. And in the absence
of eyes on us as we create, may we grow brave—nearer to ourselves.
Let us take risks that we wouldn't otherwise take and listen for our
own voice in the quiet. And in doing, may our artistry be refined
and remade. *Amen.*

FOR HONING YOUR CRAFT

Careful God,
Remind us that talent alone is never enough. Match our dreaming
with persistence, with endurance, that we would know time as a
necessary agony in order to create the kind of beauty that transcends. Help us to develop not for anyone else's affection, but for the
art's sake. Nourish our sense of purpose as artists; that as we make,
we would understand we have not only an aesthetic responsibility
but a moral one. Make us truth-tellers as you allow us to see when
those around us lack vision. And if we are to choose, let us always
choose mediocrity that communicates something true over perfec-
tion that tells a lie. Keep us from demanding too much of our present work, that we would be able to want more for what we've
created without degrading it. We are artists. In you, we claim this.
May it be so.

FOR THE ART WE'VE LOST

God of the lost gallery,
So much has been stolen from us. The work of our grandmothers' hands, of our great-grandmothers' hands, of ancestors further back still. It has been kept from us by systems that see us more as tools for production than forces of beauty. And on the occasion our creativity is recognized, it is just as soon taken—swallowed whole and put to death in the bellies of those who do not love us. May they vomit it up. May the art they've appropriated sicken them in the night. Help us to grieve every poem we will never read, every song we will never hear. The paintings, the textiles, the artifacts that have been locked up in museums for the oppressors' entertainment. What can be restored, restore. And what is dead, may it find its peace. May the ancestors walk the lost gallery, may they be moved and steadied in the arms of the poet, the painter, the sculptor. May they be taken with the glory of their own hands. *Ase.*

Breathe

INHALE: The whole earth groans.
EXHALE: Beauty is a cure.

INHALE: I am loyal to the art.
EXHALE: I free my hands.

INHALE: My imagination expands.
EXHALE: I expand with it.

Confession

Creator God,
We confess that we have confined ourselves to the binaries of analytical and artistic, logician and poet, instead of existing in the full complexity of our humanity. That which is feeling and creative we

have made optional as opposed to vital. And we destroy far more than we create. Forgive us. And in your mercy, restore our relationship to the artistry that dwells within us all. *Amen.*

Forgiveness

Let your soul receive this rest: You are remade by the same divine force that made the star and flower petal—the sacred artist who crafted you in their holy image. Mercy over you as you reclaim every beautied fragment and resurrect the creative in you. *Amen.*

Benediction

May God grant you the imagination for what could be. May your creative spark be renewed in the presence of rest and beauty, that you would not destroy yourself in order to create. And may your craft be honed with the gentle passage of time. Go in peace to create without burden. *Amen.*

Contemplation

1. Do people tend to describe you as being more logical/analytical or artistic/creative? How would it feel to be liberated from this binary? Freeing? Terrifying? Something else?
2. What is the relationship between art and truth-telling? How do you feel about Baldwin's claim that poets and artists are "the only people who know the truth about us"?
3. To create is a risk. What is at stake for you as you create? Where is there fear?
4. Explore any tensions you've experienced between artistry and self-doubt.
5. What values are central to you as you create?

6

CALLING

*I want to live the rest of my life, however long or short,
with as much sweetness as I can decently manage, loving
all the people I love, and doing as much as I can of the
work I still have to do. I am going to write fire until it
comes out of my ears, my eyes, my noseholes—everywhere.
Until it's every breath I breathe. I'm going to go out like a
fucking meteor!*   —AUDRE LORDE

"I want to fly! I want to touch the sun!"
"Finish your eggs first."   —LORRAINE HANSBERRY

LETTER VI | TO THOSE WHO DON'T
KNOW WHAT THEY'RE DOING

I've never told anyone this, but for a brief period in my twenties I
wanted to become a nun. I had been working for a small Catholic
university founded and served by an order of sisters. They were
funny and mischievous and generous and absolutely serious about
who they knew themselves to be.

It was my first time meeting a group of nuns, and in my ignorance, I'm afraid I idealized their lives. What would it mean to have
such clarity in one's calling? To live life as a vow? To rest from the
daunting task of figuring out what I'm supposed to do with each
day? I craved order. The certainty of having a time to rise and a
time to rest. The certainty of community, of provision. But more
than that, I wanted stability in my purpose. Could I choose the vow?
Would it spare me a life of anxiety and uncertainty and feeling like
my days lacked meaning? That I would die with that meaningless-
ness?

Calling, for many of us, is not a question of what we should do, but whether our lives matter at all. Perhaps believing God told us what job to choose or whom to marry has a way of imbuing our decisions with supernatural magnitude. And certainty—for if it's God who tells you, what could easily undo it? True or not, it's a kind of psychic assurance. You are not small or dithering; you have purpose.

I once asked my five-year-old nephew what he wanted to be when he grew up. He hesitated briefly and looked up at the ceiling fan as if watching for something. Then he looked down at his sticky Legos and just said, *big*. And it felt as if the exchange communicated more about me than him. For many years, I believed calling was synonymous with work. I now know it to be much more than this. It is how we will spend our days. How we help our grandmothers inch up the stairs to bed. The way we bathe ourselves in the evenings. How I hold this pen. And it is both dream and dread, for vocation does not always feel good or easy. And it may only be true for a season.

I wanted the stability of a single purpose until death; I've never cared for life in its fogginess. But calling demands that we honor its fluidity. Not all calls are eternal. They ebb and flow with us—with our needs, our community, and our loves. If there is anything static in it, it is that we are called to whatever makes us more human. Not to what makes us matter—calling has no competency in this area. Its purpose is not to prove our worth, but to show us how we might practice it. It is a divine corridor with many doors, and no one can tell you how long each door will remain unlocked. No one can save you from having to turn the knob.

I can say now that I reduced the sisters to my deepest fantasies about calling, as opposed to grasping the fullness of theirs. After all, the vow doesn't halt one's search for meaning, nor does it guarantee clarity. Sister Jean once told me that she used to want to play tennis. She thought she heard God tell her she was going to go pro, so she spent years of her life sweating and huffing under the stars at her high school's courts. But some nights on the walk home, she passed a local parish, doors wide open, and a glowing song reaching out to the sidewalk. Choir practice. One day she walked in, sat in the pew farthest away, and let herself rest in a way she rarely did. She continued to go back—mostly to make eyes at a boy she liked—but always left as quietly as she came. Until one night, she's creeping around the corner to slip out the side door and it's her racket that reaches out and touches the ankle of a deacon. An hour later, she was still there and they were still talking. It was a beginning. And soon she was picking up her rosary of her own volition.

Sister Jean rarely plays tennis anymore because of a hip that is trying its best, but she keeps a racket underneath her desk. Her feet rest on it daily. Sister Jean has many calls within her calling. Many rooms where she finds meaning, or once did. I wanted a straight line, but purpose is a landscape.

I cannot tell you what to do with your life. But I can tell you that how you spend your days is a matter of choice, place, privilege, and how willing you are to proceed down the corridor. However dimly lit. Even when your legs are trembling. If you are called to anything, it will sound like freedom. If it is meaning you are after, you will not find it on the other side of the door; it's that the doors have knobs at all.

Dreaming with you,

C

Polaris

We all know not to
Walk on the tracks
At dark,

But we are balancing bodies
On the rails to see if
It's possible

To make the shape of us
Look like a suspension
Bridge.

Someone says that isn't the North Star,
It's Venus and we close our eyes
Like a vow departing.

Someone says
Listen, listen

Even through lidded eyes
we can see lights approaching.

Prayers

FOR GOOD WORK

God of the dirt,
Reveal to us what of our work mirrors the divine. Whether teacher
or nurse, waitress or electrician, show us what virtues manifest in
our labor, how we are being formed toward goodness or destruction. We confess that we have submitted to a system where one's
compensation is entirely uncorrelated with the difficulty of one's
labor. That the janitor and the CEO receive vastly different de-
grees of respect and compensation is our collective capitalist delusion. We grieve all those who have been forced to work to survive,
those who have been bound to their exhaustion, who work two
jobs just to eat. Lay bare all the ways our society idolizes labor as
salvific when often it is killing us. Make our work more than
death to us. May we find an appropriate weight of meaning in our
occupations, that we would delight in our doing without being
reduced to our output. And if and when this balance is at stake,
help us to realign or find work that we can both honor and be
honored by. *Amen.*

FOR THOSE WHO FEEL THEIR LIVES LACK PURPOSE

Divine Intention,
We come to you having never felt a sense of purpose—nothing per-
ceivable to indicate that we were meant to be. In the absence of
projects or identities or relationships that make our lives feel important, it can feel like we are drifting. Empower us to claim our lives
both for what they are and for what we want them to be. Keep us
from comparing our days to the surface appearance of another's.
Remind us that comparison is never as innocent as it first appears,
that it claws at and mangles our concepts of achievement and relationship. Grant us the patience to withstand this hopelessness, that

we might someday look up and find intention and meaning where we thought it was void. *May it be so.*

FOR SERVICE

God of bended knee,
We kneel before you. We thank you for showing us what it means to give, not out of a desire for recognition or personal gain but out of deep humanity. Grant us compassion for all those who suffer, that our vocations would affirm the dignity of the systemically excluded and oppressed. Keep us from shallow callings that are only concerned with the self, and how we might advance in this world. Keep us from discernment that only draws us into our own interior worlds. As we make sense of our callings, may we do so with an unflinching awareness of the exterior world—the weeping of our neighbor, the groans of creation—so we would understand our vocation in relationship to those around us and their needs. Protect those who sense service and helping others as a primary call on their lives, that they would retain their empathy without allowing it to swallow them whole. May we learn to care for ourselves with equal gravity to which we care for those in our midst. *Amen.*

FOR WHEN YOU CAN'T HEAR GOD OR MAYBE NEVER HAVE

God who whispers, if at all,
If you are speaking, why not to me? I have waited. I have listened in silence, in noise, with head bowed and eyes wide open—all while wondering if you are with me. Heal the lie that you are far from any one of us. Help us to find you outside our narrow expectations for how the divine presents itself. Let us be tender with the parts of us that lack clarity and assurance. But help us to become honest that too often we are desperate for your voice because we are terrified of our own. May divine silence require us to meet ourselves— our loves, our desires, our fears—in new ways. Remind us that we

have agency, that many paths can be holy at once. And for those of us who feel that our lives lack purpose in the absence of a singular, ordained path, reveal our meaning to us daily. In the faces of those we love, in the way we are loved in return. *Amen.*

FOR THOSE WHO ARE LOOKING FOR A SIGN

God who shows,
I need a sign. However sincere my discernment, it seems like clarity continues to evade me. God, how will I know? In the absence of firm assurance, this lack of confidence pulls me here and there like a leash. Remind me that many things can be good at once, but if there is an answer that is most right for me in this season, reveal it to me. Help me to have compassion for myself as I name my uncertainty. Show me what it means to be a person of both conviction and openness, that I might gain the courage to act and decide even when it feels like a risk. May I find divine affirmation on the path to self-trust. *Amen.*

Breathe

INHALE: To love and be loved.
EXHALE: My purpose remains.

INHALE: I don't know what my path is.
EXHALE: But I am led into freedom.

INHALE: I listen for the divine.
EXHALE: My soul whispers back.

Confession

Present God,
We confess that we have made our callings into puzzles we must solve in order for our lives to have meaning. We have reduced vocation to labor and forgotten what it means to be called to virtue, and even love. We have falsely made our dignity dependent on our work

and fallen prey to the lie that to hear you is to be near to you. Have mercy on us and forgive us, that we might be liberated into our path in its own time. *Amen.*

Forgiveness

Let your soul receive this rest: The divine presence remains near as you locate the path that feels right to you. Receive forgiveness and be guided into your deepest longings and beliefs as you decide how to spend your days. When self-distrust begins to eclipse your callings, let God steady you toward what is good and true and beautiful, now and forever. *Amen.*

Benediction

Now listen to the sounds that stir within, listen to the cries for help that ring around you, and follow a path of healing and liberation for you and all you encounter. Take peace in the sound of your own voice as you choose the life that honors your truest self. *May it be so.*

Contemplation

1. Is there a calling that you feel is primary in your life (work, family, service, play, love)? Explore a story of how that came to be.
2. What do you believe about communication with the divine? Is it clear and directive or curious and open-ended? Does it occur through language? Feeling and intuition? How does this affect your sense of calling?
3. How does your sense of self interfere with your sense of calling? What are the hidden longings and loves that drive you?
4. What do you daydream about? What of your dreaming speaks to how you want to spend your days? How do you discern if a dream has merit or is a form of escapism?
5. How does anxiousness affect your relationship with vocation? What words of assurance can you speak over yourself today?

7

BODY

I believed, and still do, that our bodies are our selves, that my soul is the voltage conducted through neurons and nerves, and that my spirit is my flesh.

—TA-NEHISI COATES

I have the uncanny feeling that, just at the end of my life, I am beginning to reinhabit completely the body I long ago left.

—ALICE WALKER

LETTER VII | TO BODIES

I wonder how this letter comes to you. Are you hunched over these pages, neck severed from shoulders that are rounded from the weight of you? Do they come to you through earphones or a laptop as you're wrist-deep in dish suds or driving a car you forgot you were driving at all?

I do my best listening in the fetal position, and I do my best writing in the dark. Tonight, it's both. I've been typing with my eyes closed to save them from the computer light. If my hands misalign just slightly, the words become gibberish. Everything has a cost.

Whatever has been making me sick for the past six years has moved into my eyes, making it hard to focus on light. Of the many eye conditions I've been diagnosed with in recent years, convergence insufficiency is the least worrisome yet most inconvenient. My eyes aren't cooperating. Quite literally, they just can't seem to work together anymore. The nerves in the muscles surrounding them are not communicating well, and the muscles themselves have grown weak and atrophied. When I close my eyes, the pupils shoot to the far corners of my eye sockets, and when I open them, they pull and tug like hell to find their way back to center. My doctor says my body is in fight-or-flight mode—from the illness or maybe further back still. The eyes being unable to converge is apparently an evolutionary response to needing to see a wider frame in the presence of a threat. Only it's 2:16 A.M. and there is no threat to be found. Someone should tell my eyes. I need my parasympathetic nervous system to reclaim its space and guide my body back into rest again, though when I call upon it, it rarely answers.

I know I shouldn't blame myself for this, but it's vexing that I can't just will myself to relax, that my body no longer enters rest like it should. I meditate and I spend mornings in silence, and I've constructed a dozen tiny habits in hopes of calming myself. But the stress of existing in a body that has felt like a stranger in recent years is enough to make anyone's shoulders tense.

Last year, a neurologist called me disabled for the first time. Until then, the thought had never occurred to me. Monday, as I was walking by the lake with a friend, I used the language myself and she stared back at me in horror. *Well, you won't stay like this,* she said. *This won't be forever.* I cannot say for certain that she meant it this way, but it was as if my coming to terms with the body I now occupied was a threat to her perception of me. I had to wonder, If I did "stay" like this, what would that mean to her? Was it pity she felt? Grief?

At thirty-two, I'm still learning to live life in a disabled body, just as my six-year-old self had to learn to live life in a Black body and my twelve-year-old self in a queer body. And I am unlearning what I've been taught—that I'm lazy, ugly, dirty. That I'm unwanted. That my skin and flesh are a burden. Remaining in denial about this body, being held captive to a notion that it will surely heal, no longer serves me in my love for it. I have had to learn to extend welcome to my eyes. To become a creature of unflinching hospitality to every new ache and twitch. Not that I would lose hope for a life with less pain, but that I would not drift too far from the present one. Because that distance, between what I crave my body to be and what it is, so quickly becomes the path to disembodiment and then, despairingly, to self-hatred in all forms.

Maybe you've known what it is to leave your body to survive. And maybe when the threat has subsided, you've been unable to find your way back. This racist, capitalist, ableist world does not want to keep you whole. It can only stand to benefit from bodies emptied of their protectors. But hear this: If you aren't in your body, someone else is. You will too soon find that the many tyrants of the world have taken the helm in your absence. For this reason, our liberation practice must be tied to a reclamation of the physical self—to an embodied homecoming. Just as our spiritualities draw us into our interior worlds, they should also be a map back home to our bodies, a mirror held to our very faces.

Whose mouth is this, whose hands are these? Hands that tremble, eyes that dart in all directions. Whose neck is this, tall and unbowed? *Welcome.* You are safe here. *Welcome.* Your body is good.

In the flesh,

C

resurrection

Climb back inside
Your body
No more split
Selves
Minds without
Skulls
Thirst without
Tongues—flail and
shake like a haunting
You are alive

Prayers

FOR THE MIRROR

God of all flesh,
God of these hips, this nose, these lips. God of fat bodies, disabled bodies, aging bodies. God of Black bodies, glistening like the mirror itself. Speak over our flesh now: Our bodies are good. We have endured all manner of antagonism. We have been trained in a singular, white-exalting form of beauty. Grant us an enduring belief in our own loveliness, but keep us from punishing ourselves on the days we feel that we do not have access to that belief. Remind us that we are doing the best we can to love ourselves in a world that breeds self-hatred. And let us remember that our beauty is never dependent on anyone's belief in it, including our own. This flesh, this face is inherently sacred—its beauty cannot easily be undone. Show us daily the miracle of these bodies that pump blood, shed tears, keep breathing. Remind us that we are those whose flesh grows back, that we possess the mystery of regeneration within our bones. Give us the courage to marvel, every mirror a portal to the awe we are worthy of. *Ase.*

FOR THOSE WHO LEFT THEIR BODIES TO SURVIVE

Divine Protector,
Remind us that our bodies are sacred. The stories we've inherited, of both beauty and trauma, rest on our bones. We have known what it is to have our physical agency stolen from us. We have known what it is to have our bodies used more than loved. And each day, capitalism demands we sacrifice blood and muscle at its altar. We betray our physical selfhood to survive, yet leaving it behind is a greater death still. As we long for justice and deeper liberation, train us to listen well to our flesh; that we would make, eat, drink,

rest, weep, stretch, move in freedom, knowing that our bodies are not enemy but sacred guardians of our glory. *May it be so.*

FOR THE DISABLED AND CHRONICALLY ILL

God of every ache,

Help us to befriend our bodies. We confess that it is easy to turn against them as the source of our struggle. Awaken a compassion, a tenderness, toward the parts of us that are changing or hurting, remembering that our bodies are doing everything they can to protect us. That our bodies are fighting, are trying their best to hold back the pain and exhaustion. And with every ailing and unseen thing, guide us toward those capable of listening and perceiving when we are not okay, that we wouldn't feel pressure to pretend or apologize or explain but could exist in the truth of what we need. Remind us that we are not a burden but a beacon to those who are so poorly attuned to their own bodies and needs that they have forgotten what self-compassion looks like. Hold us in love as we resist the demands of this world. *May it be so.*

FOR QUEER BODIES

Strange God,

Thank you for reminding us it is okay to be incomprehensible—to be creatures of mystery and fluidity. Be near to us as we grieve the ways we've been pressured to conform to who others wish us to be. Renew us as we resist the temptation to perform an embodiment that isn't true to us. But help us to have compassion for ourselves when it seems as if enacting a charade is the only way to be safe and loved. Grant us an interior clarity that is unwavering in the face of transphobia and homophobia, that we might withstand every critique and dismissal, the overt and the passive-aggressive. Help us to travel into those stories of feeling alienated in our own bodies and return back to ourselves with dignity crying out from every bone.

We reject the lie that our bodies are bad. We rebuke the lie that we are dirty. And we honor our truest voice, our self-knowledge as central to our own making and remaking. Against hope, we have found a way to hear the truth of us amid the vitriol of this world. May these queer bodies be a beacon to a world in bondage to its own binaries; may our flesh liberate the world into embodied attunement. *Amen.*

FOR WOMEN RECLAIMING THEIR BODIES

Sacred Feminine One,
We are grateful that you have granted us identity in our womanness. That you exist in a multitude that includes the feminine is deeply affirming in a world that diminishes and dismisses female contribution while consuming our bodies. Protect us from the threats that lurk, that follow too closely behind on the sidewalk, that ask us to smile on cue. Protect us from misogyny's every whim, that we would be released from the anxiety of life in a woman body. Reveal to us the distinct glory that resides in us. We want time with ourselves in awe of ourselves, God. Help us to marvel at those of us who can hold and birth life, but also remind us womanhood is not defined by the womb. Remind us of our strength and our softness, our emotions and our strategy, and the long line of women from whom we descend, who knew their worth and existed in it without compromise. *Amen.*

FOR AGING BODIES

Ancient God,
It is difficult to remain embodied when our bodies are awake with new aches and ways of being. Whose hands are these? Trembling and spotted. Whose eyes are these? Graying and blurred. These bodies are not the ones we once knew. We are constantly meeting ourselves anew, and we confess that it grows difficult to extend wel-

come. We thank you for being a God who is both young and old. Who has traveled through many years, but still possesses a passion for life. Teach us to remember the dignity of our age, that our years would speak to the wisdom and depth of us. Liberate us from a singular portrait of ourselves as youthful, that we would spit out the ageism that society attempts to feed us daily. Instill in us a sense of protection over these bodies which have done so much for us over the years—bodies that wept for us, that danced, that breathed, that carried us to this moment. May we grant them the honor they are due. *Amen.*

Breathe

INHALE: I can listen to my body.
EXHALE: I will stay whole.

INHALE: My body is good.
EXHALE: I will not abandon it.

INHALE: This flesh is divine.
EXHALE: The physical is the spiritual.

Confession

Embodied God,

We confess that we have rent mind from matter, been deceived into viewing our bodies as tools for productivity as opposed to sacred beings worthy of love and honor. In our spiritualities, we have exalted the invisible over the physical. In our daily routines, we have not cared for our bodies well. And that neglect has rippled out toward the bodies of others in our midst. Forgive us, God, and restore in us a sacred attunement to our whole selves—minds, blood, breath, the hands that grip these pages. With divine help, may we never abandon ourselves again. *Amen.*

Forgiveness

Let your soul receive this rest: The same God who knit together the physical realm has mercy on your body today. Trust that you can be relieved of any guilt for a body that doesn't perform or appear or exist in the way others demand. Be assured that your body is good as it is, forgiven that you would remain whole and embodied, with shame forever far from you. *Amen.*

Benediction

With the power of the God who comes in flesh for all flesh, go in courage to remain in your body, that you would stay whole in a world content to see you torn apart. *May it be so.*

Contemplation

1. How do you feel about your body today? What part of it are you proud of? Which part needs extra protection?
2. When you're stressed, what aspect of bodily care are you prone to forget first? What is one habit you can implement to resist this?
3. When was the last time you felt in awe of your body?
4. Take five minutes in stillness to listen to your body. What do you feel and where?
5. What words of compassion can you speak over your body today?

8

BELONGING

Without community, there is no liberation, only the most vulnerable and temporary armistice between an individual and her oppression. —AUDRE LORDE

There are two questions that [we] must ask [ourselves]. The first is "Where am I going?" and the second is "Who will go with me?" If you ever get these questions in the wrong order, you are in trouble.

—HOWARD THURMAN

The world is not a pleasant place
to be without
someone to hold and be held by.

—NIKKI GIOVANNI

LETTER VIII | TO LONELY FORAGERS

I'm writing to you as one who used to lie about having friends on the playground. As one who bent her voice an octave higher so people would think her more charming than sullen. I'm writing to you as the one who was too afraid to leave. Who stayed because the distance to the door was too great without someone to be held by. At the core of me, and I suspect humanity, is a hunger to belong. Or at least the defiant sting of never belonging. You know this haunt, but I wonder if you've been able to become honest about it.

There is something inherently vulnerable about saying you want to belong. For, to name you are lonely, and then be met with nothing, only doubles the loneliness. It is much easier to construct illusions around your "independence" and solitariness. To admit your desire to be known would mean acknowledging the shame asleep in you that says you aren't worth knowing—the doubt that says they cannot be trusted to love you.

I'm beginning to think alienation and rejection are the two great persuaders of our own unloveliness. The cunning will wield them against you so that you acquiesce to the systems of a community in order to retain membership in it. Perhaps you know what it's like to need to believe a certain doctrine or creed so that you can belong in a spiritual space, or to vote a certain way to belong at the dinner table. When someone places your very belonging at stake, they are prodding an ancient wound. Not all belonging is salve.

For you, I want more. I want friendship, romance, family. I want a community that will not destroy you. I want belonging that isn't always at risk, that isn't always being threatened. For you, I want the sense of self required to walk away, to forage for solid bonds. To be known is not frivolous; it is survival. You will not survive by self-care and self-love alone. Who will hold you? Who will remember you? You, who are something to behold. You, who are flawed and mysterious and needy and good.

Belonging is not too great an ask. Find your sacred company. And may they find and cherish you.

With you,

C

Covalence

Someday I will join them, this table
of women with folds in their cheeks and calico floral to
their ankles, mumbling and purring at the sizzle of
a voice through the radio,
graying eyes conveying, bidding all the way to game.
A single pendant rests above, no light dispersing
beyond their hands. These women
who take up the bone to each other's teeth and make sure
nothing's there that shouldn't be.

In all places

Listen

For the way

Your breath sounds

As it escapes

You.

Prayers

FOR OLD FRIENDS

God who remembers,
We're grateful for the friends who've stayed. In a world of so much relational transitivity, it is no small miracle to retain a sense of connection across years. We thank you for those who have held us through tragedy and grief—who've borne witness to our tear-streaked faces and waited with us in the dark. Those who have witnessed the good, the healing, and been there to toast to the triumphs of this life. Those who have seen us in the mundane—the brunches, the flat tires, the long hours, our voices changing. We thank you for showing us that some loves last. That we are worthy of a belonging that transcends circumstance. Protect these bonds, that we would not grow bitter or disillusioned with one another. Or, if disillusionment is our fate, may it be because we can love apart from the mirage of one another's goodness, or niceness, or brilliance. Let ours be a company that has no need for such enchantments. And, having seen one another face-to-face, give us the courage to remain. *May it be so.*

FOR LOST FRIENDS

God of endings,
It is difficult to fade from those who we once felt known by. Help us to remember that the end of friendship does not negate what once was—that it's okay to diverge, and that there are times when a friendship lost is nothing less than the result of someone's liberation, someone living into another calling. Remind us of the beauty of things that only last for a season. Grant us space to grieve that end. And if the end is not peaceable, grant us space to heal, that our appetites for good friendship would not wane, but that we would press on toward a new kind of belonging. *Amen.*

FOR VULNERABILITY

God of the untold,

Protect us. Too often, we have had our pain used to make other people feel like they have achieved the farce of intimacy. We are weary of communal spaces that ask us to bare ourselves for their sake, without ever becoming thoughtful about how they will care for us in the wake of our exposure. Reveal these moments as fleeting sentimentality and protect us from their draw. Liberate us from the lie that vulnerability is an accurate portrait of relational goodness. Remind us that some stories aren't meant for everyone, and that is good and okay. If we open ourselves to others, may it only be in the presence of those who are capable keepers of our true selves. And in the presence of those who are more interested in using us to rouse emotion in their emptiness, help us to choose ourselves, our wholeness; that we would practice a sacred withholding that mirrors the one who made us. *Amen.*

FOR LONELY SOULS

Near God,

Thank you for being a God who does not wish for us to be alone. We hold close that you are a God who didn't just feed the five thousand, but gave them people to eat with. We confess that we've become so acquainted with rejection that we struggle to believe when others truly want to be with us. Keep us from pushing them away. Grant us the discernment and belief to allow others to stay, that we would never become too familiar with loneliness. As we find ourselves in seasons of doubt and disappointment, let us encounter the face of God in the faces of those who love us. And when we feel ourselves drawn toward a person or place, help us to perceive if our longing is rushing us toward those who are unsafe or incapable of loving us well. We long to be chosen, to be known and understood. Heal the stories of abandonment and rejection buried in us. And draw near to the lonely as we find our people. *Amen.*

FOR THE BLACK SHEEP OF THE FAMILY

God of black sheep,
It wasn't easy alone—to be so distinct from our families that we questioned our belonging. We admit that at times it has been easier to construct narratives about our own independence and uniqueness than contend with the pain of being left out and misunderstood. Draw us near to our child selves. The child who wanted to be embraced, who wanted to be remembered and have their selfhood taken seriously. Help us to lavish on ourselves the honor withheld from us in our youth. Let us learn the sound of our voices, not as discord but as beauty. In the absence of familial harmony, may we at least have this—an assurance that we, however queer or distinct, are still beloved. That we are worthy of a belonging that does not demand uniformity but understands and honors our stunning particularity. *Ase.*

FOR BEING KNOWN

Divine Community,
We want to be known and we're terrified of being known. Of being laid bare in the presence of another. We are grateful that you are not a God who demands a spirituality rooted in some solitary existence, but it is hard to belong without allowing the direction of our lives to be dictated by those from whom we seek affirmation. Help us to daily discern the truth of our selfhood, that our communities would offer insight without commanding assimilation. As we find spaces that truly see and know us, help us to not run from them. The more beautiful a thing is, the more terrified we are of losing it. Do not let this terror keep us from the love we were meant for. And as we learn to accept friendship and care, may we be stirred to extend it to others. Keep us from contributing to loneliness and dislocation in the world, knowing that our freedom is mysteriously entwined with the freedom of those around us. *Amen.*

FOR WHEN YOU NEED TO BE FREED FROM A FRIEND

God who left,

We are heavy with relational doubt, never certain if we are truly known or loved. Friendship laced with skepticism leaves us lonely even in crowds. We have been forgotten, compared, uninvited. We've been kept around and used to make others feel superior. Help us to sense and walk away from poisoned belonging, knowing it is not our duty to make our friendship available for the plundering of any wanderer. Grant us that wisdom which tells us when to stay and when to find new people to trust with our souls. Help us to reimagine friendship; that we would want more for ourselves than relationships that secretly center envy and image, those that make belonging a prize to be won. Draw us closer to those whose love and dreaming for us are rooted in sacred mutuality—the belief that we are not just welcomed but that we are vital to the life and beauty of the collective. Even as we evolve, as we apprehend our true selves, may our standing in the collective always be sure. Let who we are becoming be honored in the place where we are, or be with us as we depart. *Amen.*

Breathe

INHALE: I was meant for love.
EXHALE: God, help me to receive it.

INHALE: I need more than me.
EXHALE: We get free together.

INHALE: I am worthy of embrace.
EXHALE: God, lead me to belonging.

Confession

God of welcome,

We confess that at times we have been content to exclude or neglect those our communities cannot *use*. We have been so wrapped up in status and symbol that we have constructed walls not out of wisdom or self-understanding, but out of feigned superiority and elitism. We have not loved well. We have prioritized the powerful and popular. We have neglected the friends who give more than they ever receive. We have forgotten the quiet. We have forgotten ourselves. Have mercy on us, that we might become faithful harbors for belonging in a dislocated world. And as we gaze on the faces of the lonely, of the abandoned, forgive us. *Amen.*

Forgiveness

Let your soul receive this rest: The God whose friends fell asleep in the garden on the night he needed them desperately has mercy on you now. Just as this sacred company rose to be loved by God evermore, may you also know and receive this same forgiveness, extending it to all whom you've chosen to love and be loved by. *Amen.*

Benediction

May the God who exists in a multitude lead you into communities of true belonging. May they protect you from spaces that demand a selfhood that is no longer true of you and guide you toward those who can glimpse your true face. May God preserve those friendships that are meant to last, and may they grant you the stability of heart to let go when the time has come to find belonging elsewhere. And to the lonely, the isolated, may the divine be company to you as you wait for the embrace you are worthy of. Go in peace, one sacred soul in a collective. *Amen.*

Contemplation

1. Who was the first friend you felt deeply known by? Were they known by you in return? How was intimacy cultivated?
2. What communities are you currently grounded in? How do or don't they understand you?

3. Travel into a memory of being rejected by someone you wanted to be accepted by. How did this form you? In what ways is loneliness real to you in this season?

4. How do you respond to alienation and rejection in your life? What habits of coping (for better and worse) are practiced in the aftermath?

9

DOUBT

The betrayal of a belief is not the same thing as ceasing to believe.   —JAMES BALDWIN

Even the silence
has a story to tell you.
Just listen. Listen.
                                        —JACQUELINE WOODSON

LETTER IX | TO THOSE WHO CAN'T HEAR
OVER THE WAVES

I am five or six and my father has taken me and my sister out to eat at Denny's. We box up much of our meal to-go, including my untouched glass of milk. The server pours it into one of those plastic kids' cups with the built-in lid and flexi straw. You know the kind, the outside decorated with mazes or cartoons. And as Arthur family lore goes, when we get into the car, I begin a very long interrogation of the cup's contents. *How do I know it's milk?* I ask. And my father says, *Because I'm telling you it's milk.* I say, *But I can't see that it's milk,* inspecting the opaque vessel. *Nicole, I'm telling you it's milk.* I ask, *But how do you know it's milk?* Eventually my father pries open the lid and shows me the milk inside. It's white. It looks like milk. But still. *It could be something else white.* This went on for more time than I'm sure my twenty-four-year-old single father had the energy for, until eventually we just gave the cup to my sister who slurped it up happily as I watched (with maybe some tinge of jealousy or regret). So, when my family says I was born a skeptic, I don't argue.

You may be wondering how it came to be that a six-year-old could lack such trust in how the world presented itself. I'm afraid I learned too early that people aren't precisely who they appear to be. How much of my skepticism was inherent and how much was the product of trauma, I cannot say. But I admire my father's patience with my unbelief, his attempts to move me toward trust without forcing me to drink. Perhaps he knew my leeriness would someday protect me. Sometimes distrust of the world means you are learning to trust yourself.

I've just finished Octavia Butler's *Parable of the Sower* again. In it a fifteen-year-old Black girl named Lauren has the self-trust to name her own God. Her father is a pastor in a more traditional Christian context, and on the edge of apocalypse, she recognizes that his religion is not for her. She understands its complicity in the end of her world—the degradation of land, the walled neighborhoods that the privileged have erected to keep the poor out. She feels that she can no longer approach that kind of religion with self-honesty. She writes, "My God has another name," and goes on to realize a new form for the divine in her life.

You would not be alone if you found the thought of a child unveiling a new religion a bit terrifying. But even in the terror of it, there is something beautiful about a child possessing the courage to make meaning out of profound devastation. That instead of relinquishing her connection to the divine, she would seek a God of more mystery and healing than she had been given access to. That she would make her own cup to drink from.

Years after the milk incident, I would be baptized in dirty waters off the shore of Ocean City, Maryland. I had situated myself in Christian spaces in college, culminating in a job in collegiate ministry after I graduated. Before going under, I had to answer a series of questions. "Do you wholly trust in Jesus Christ as your Lord and Savior?" And I felt my throat tighten as I whispered over the waves, *Yes.* "Do you turn from Satan and all his ways in obedience to Jesus?" I didn't know, but I nodded and said, *I do.* The waves were so loud, I could barely hear my own voice.

Maybe I thought the water would change me. That the words would *become* true as I enacted the ritual. But when I emerged from the water, I was just cold and disoriented. The waves crashed against my back, and I dragged myself to shore.

I can say now that my baptism was beautiful not because it was true, but because it led me to contend with a charade of self. This is what I wrote after I came home that night:

> I don't know why I said yes today. It felt like I had to with everyone already waiting on the beach watching me. I'm glad they couldn't hear anything. My lie was only heard by God. If there is a God. I don't know. I don't know anything. But I never claimed to want to know. Is everyone just faking it? Was I just baptized into a grand and coordinated lie? Or is this what belief will always look like for me?

Much of my skepticism is born of an unhealthy distrust, but maybe some of it is also born of wisdom. Often when we demand that someone be sure or think the same thing about God as us, it is because we are terrified to confront our own doubts. We experience their liberation as a threat. In this way, religious certainty can be seen as a product of white supremacy. The tyrant thrives on subjugation, survives by a lack of questioning. By people who act and believe (or say they believe) without challenging those in power.

If your belonging depends on whether you ascribe to the beliefs of a spiritual leader, it is not belonging, it is bondage. When someone's friendships and community are at stake, how can they be expected to become curious or honest with themselves in their own spiritual exploration? I am convinced the vast majority of evangelical Christians are feigning belief in oppressive doctrines because they are terrified of being cast out of their communities, of losing loved ones. On mission to retain their belonging, we encourage them to deceive even themselves.

I no longer demand belief where there is tension. If the divine is all-knowing, I suspect they understand why I find it difficult to believe in a God who's loving or kind or listening at all in a world of so much sorrow and injustice. Our doubts are credible. Our disbelief, human. And I see no need for us to force one another to resolve them under the false promise of salvation or nearness to God. I'm not a person of certainty. It is not a *lack of* conviction that I feel, rather a complete conviction of divine mystery. I've never heard the voice of God. I've never felt them calling out to me in the pits of despair. I don't know what I think about the Trinity, and I don't know a thing about heaven or hell or the in-between. I know that trees die and come back to life and it's beautiful, and the right sunset steadies my breath. I know that my sister will answer when I call, and she'll always take the first sip when I don't trust the milk. I know my name and the sound of my gramma's voice speaking it. Maybe this is what belief will always look like for me. Fragments of beauty at rest with divine mystery. "My God has another name."

With doubt,

C

Like Jesus to the Crows

by Vievee Francis

that gathered there along his arms,
upon the invitation of a slender limb.
And not oblivious to human violence
perhaps needed rest or needed to offer
the succor of presence, despite the
stiff collar of their feathers, despite
each one being no less the children
of a father who claimed an upper realm.

It is not true they pecked his eyes. Nor
did they consider his wounds
their own. They were neither irreverent
nor quiet. They spoke in the tongues
they knew. They cawed full voiced
and would have released him from his
bindings had their beaks held the power
and had there been time in that place.

Like them, I have sought to comfort and
so be comforted. Like them
I have seen the failure of miracles when
they were most needed. Like Him, I
have called upon those so unlike myself
when my father failed to answer.

Prayers

FOR THOSE WHO ARE FEIGNING CERTAINTY

God of uncertain souls,

We are tired of pretending. For too long we have declared belief in things that grate against our very souls. We have recited creeds and doctrines, we have regurgitated facts and passages, all in hopes of placating the gnawing doubts that dwell deep within us. We have been manipulated and baited by song, story, and teacher into thinking there is a singular approach to the divine. Liberate us from the tyranny of spiritual certainty. Remind us that doubt is not a threat to faith; it is faith that has finally taken off its mask. Help us locate what of the divine feels clear and true to us. And help us to become honest about those things that will always remain a sacred question. Hold us close to you as we diverge from the path laid out by others, that we might find you in the unknown of the tall grass, the reeds, and even the wilderness—at home with mystery in your divine labyrinth. *May it be so.*

FOR AGNOSTICS

Unknowable God,

We do not know to whom we pray—or why we pray, when the truth is we are creatures of uncertainty. If there is any truth to the divine, may it be that you are loving and kind and disinterested in how much belief I am able to muster on any given day. If there is love in you, may it be a love that remains near even when the one you love is oblivious to your nearness. God, if you're near, would you protect us and keep us? Keep us from ever being too proud to ask this. And if our prayers are spoken into the void, may we find healing and self-knowledge as we hear our words ourselves. That in them we would encounter our deepest longings and fears, and be compelled to ask for help, however uncertain that help may be. May we live in protection of the unknown, that we would reserve the right to be curious, open, content with the mysteries of the cosmos, even if that does not preclude us from praying these words now. *May it be so.*

FOR THOSE WHO THOUGHT THEY KNEW

God of belief,
When we take account of the tragedies of the world, it is difficult to believe there is a powerful and loving God with us. There is so much we wish you would intervene in to bring justice and healing now. We trust that you are a God who is patient with these doubts. A God who is not threatened by our unbelief but draws near to us in it. Help us toward an understanding of you that includes tension and mystery. Let us be empathetic with our souls, which have endured so much suffering, and incline us to ask deep questions of our maker. But as we do so, let us find an empathy for you—a God who is no stranger to suffering but endures all things with us—that we might find full liberation. Let our doubts lead us into deeper intimacy with the divine as we tell the truth of the questions that plague us. *Amen.*

FOR THOSE WHO'VE NEVER FELT GOD

God of Thomas,
We are grateful that you are not made insecure or agitated by our disbelief. Instead, you show us great compassion, understanding how difficult it is to believe without meeting God face-to-face. As we are confronted with the tragedies and traumas of our current moment, we need you—a Christ with dark and scarred flesh—to bare your wounds and let us press our own scarred flesh into yours, so that we can remember a God who knew suffering. A God of true solidarity. In the face of our deepest doubts, thank you for moving

closer. Grant that as we draw near to the wounds of those we love, we might somehow touch the wounds of Christ and find belief. *Amen.*

FOR THOSE WHO DON'T TRUST SPIRITUAL SPACES

God of wisdom,

It's hard to know what to say to a God claimed by those who have wounded us. Can we trust you? We have known what it is to exist in spiritual spaces that are more interested in controlling us than loving us. To have the room turn against us when our beliefs diverge from the group's. We thank you for giving us an interior compass, an intuition that no longer trusts spirituality that feels like captivity. Free us from those spaces. But as we depart, keep us from relinquishing our own connection to the divine. Help us to approach you slowly in the safety of our own interior worlds before granting another spiritual space access to us. And when we're ready, guide us into new and safe communities—communities capable of holding our deepest doubts, our beliefs, the fullness of uncertainty, without being threatened. May we approach shrewdly and carefully, for our own protection, as we search for spaces that honor the whole of us. *Ase.*

Breathe

INHALE: I am free to not know.
EXHALE: I can rest in mystery.

INHALE: I may not know what I believe,
EXHALE: but I know it will sound like dignity.

INHALE: My doubts are sacred.
EXHALE: God, stay close as I wander.

Confession

God who is near,
We confess that we have demanded certainty from the mystery of
you. We have pressured one another toward clarity when, in truth,
we often do not know what we believe or think. We have made you
into a caricature that is easy to digest as opposed to a divine, cosmic
force. We elevate our own intellect, terrified to become honest about
the limitations of the human imagination. Forgive us our arrogance, that we might be graciously led into the abiding mystery of
the divine, and in mystery find true rest. *Amen.*

Forgiveness

Let your soul receive this rest: The divine who is both visible and
invisible, near and far, small and grand, has mercy on you. Allow
them to liberate you from the bondage of certainty, that you would
walk freely into curiosity, imagination, and a sacred unknowing.
Amen.

Benediction

May the God who allowed Thomas to press into his wounds guide
your hands toward a belief that is compassionate and tender. May
you be protected from the tyranny of certainty and breathe in divine mystery daily. *Amen.*

Contemplation

1. How has doubt been received in the spiritual spaces you've belonged to?
2. What in your story makes it hard for you to believe in the divine?
   Is clarity important to you?
3. Explore a time when you felt pressured to pretend you were cer-

tain of something you were in fact unsure of. What motivates you to pretend in spiritual spaces?

4. Explore the relationship between mystery and fear in you. What fears drive you toward certainty?

5. What words of compassion can you offer yourself about an area of disbelief (be it spiritual doubt, self-doubt, or an inability to believe in goodness in the world around you)?

1 0

LAMENT

You cry when you're born because your lungs expand. You breathe. I think that's really kind of significant. You come into the world crying, and it's a sign that you're alive.

—JAMAICA KINCAID

The condition of truth is to allow suffering to speak.

—CORNEL WEST

But this grief, for all its awful weight, insists that he matters.

—JESMYN WARD

LETTER X | TO THOSE TOO QUICK
TO WIPE AWAY THE TEARS

I should tell you I've been sad for as long as I can remember—long enough that some days I wonder if I even know sadness at all. Have you ever said the same word over and over again until it's unrecognizable coming from your mouth? You can become so familiar with something that your familiarity renders it foreign. I don't know if I am the person to write this letter to you.

A few months ago, I was going through old journals from childhood. I was looking for the first short story I ever wrote, and instead found poems by childhood Cole describing how she doesn't want to exist anymore. The first entry of this kind was from 1998. I was eight years old. I've no memory of writing any of them, or even of being aware of death in this way. Now thirty-two, I sit at my kitchen table with pages face down. I begin starting and erasing messages to a friend, attempting to translate the pages to them. I take pictures of the pages. I delete them. I start a solemn text. I start a witty text. But with every draft, the cost of sharing grows larger. *Is this*

what "trauma dumping" is? Will they feel like they need to find
something wise to say? Does it seem like I just want attention? Does it
even matter at all if it was so long ago?

In the end, I send two lines from a poem accompanied by a joke.
This is from eleven-year-old Cole:

> I hate that everyday I wear this veil and watched detached,
> and yet overwhelmed with emotion and I want nothing
> more than to scream.
> I hate that I'm sitting here feeling alone and repulsive and
> have an itching to walk out on life altogether for this reason.

Send. But with a joke about being a prodigy at cursive and how
the hell I knew the word *repulsive* as an eleven-year-old. The
phone rings and I regret it all. I normally wouldn't answer, but it
feels cruel not to, and I don't want him to think I'm feeling exactly
what I am feeling. I brace myself for whatever pity or awkward
words of comfort he has assembled. But when I pick up, there is
just silence.

I don't know how to explain the difference between a silence
that is judgmental or awkward and one that is tender, but when
you live it, you know. We listen to each other breathing, a compassionate silence stretching out in the space between us. To the silence, I say, *I know.* And I don't know what I know. A few more
moments pass, and he says, *If you're going to keep reading, set me*
down next to you. He says, *You don't have to read them out loud. I'll*
just be here.

What does it mean to be present to the pain of another? How do
we keep ourselves from rushing to trite platitudes and promises
that we have no right to utter? We must become honest about the
fact that usually when we are attempting to resolve someone else's
pain, it is not for their comfort, it is for our own. But what happens
when you remind a friend you aren't afraid of their pain? How will
you behold their suffering without reducing them to it? Two friends
miles apart sitting at the kitchen table listening to each other's

breath, and there is no resolve. Only the tender silence of everything we don't have words for.

Maybe you were taught that sadness is more dangerous than liberating. But healing comes when we are at last able to point to
where it hurts. Lament is not a threat to our survival but a means to
it. It's how hope's salve knows where to go.

Still, it would be irresponsible of me to guide you into lament
without a caution. There is a difference between lament and despair. This distinction is vital. You are so much more than your pain.
And the world, for all its terror, is awake with tremendous beauty.
We cannot allow sorrow to become any more real to us than the
glory of the night sky, the laughter around our kitchen tables. Lament should be an invitation, not an unwelcome guest.

I tell you this because there are forms for sadness that survive in
the mouth of despair. A kind of sadness that does not want you
well, because it cares more for its own survival than yours. Do not
let your grief become a locked door. You must carefully and slowly
allow others to enter.

Social media, for better or worse, has granted us entrance to the
pain of the world in ways we might otherwise be obtuse to. But
most days we can scroll from great tragedy to great tragedy without
feeling or processing it in any meaningful way. Our grief has been
expedited as we are thrust into and ripped from expressions of sorrow with the flick of our thumb. If we are to endure the weight of
such access, we must learn truer habits of emotional attunement.
Otherwise, our efforts of solidarity with the suffering will become
an interior quicksand.

When you practice lament with intentionality, you claim agency
in your own emotional life. It's not a sinking, it's a steadying. You
light the candle on the altar for the one you lost. You linger in your
parked car, letting that song move you. You cry and don't apologize
for it. You tell stories. You name exactly what has been stolen.

This is my apology to you: You are no burden. You shouldn't have
had to rush through your grief. You should never have had to sit
through thoughtless pep talks or trite and over-spiritualized words

about "hoping in God." You deserve more than that. I wish you had no reason to grieve, but now that it's arrived at your door, I pray that you open it. I hope its stay looks how you need it to. You are no further from the divine because of your pain. With every wail, you become more human. Every ache, an admission that something mattered. Until you're ready, don't let them wipe away a single tear.

Love,

C

translation

1.

None of you speak
The same language
As your
Father anymore.
At dinner you call green
Onions chives and sweet
Potatoes yams.
By the time
You think to pray,
He's already
said amen
And there's still no knives in this house.

2.

Your twin
Bed is speaking
And it reminds you how
much you heard
from upstairs
when a stranger
wept below,
And it sounds too familiar
Not to
Bury yourself into the pillow
You haven't covered yet.

3.

He waits for everyone
In the morning with mud already

Wet on his boots.
You eat your eggs sunny side up, no it's over
Easy. Everyone walks together
To the mahogany
Casket that was the only one
Left.

4.

And when his body crumples
Into something you've never
Seen, and when you don't know
how to hold someone who's only ever held
try to find his face
In the carpet fibers
Where he
buried himself twice

5.

Feel the body shake.
Brace the wood against your palm
Place the wail on your sagging tongue
As the room becomes strange
And familiar
Baptized in the tears of someone you never even met.

Prayers

FOR THOSE WHO HAVE FORGOTTEN HOW TO CRY

God of the unmoved,
Move our spirits. Whether out of trauma or pride, some of us have
left our emotions in our past or have turned against them altogether. We feel safer in our stoicism, protected from looking the
fool, from the risk of doubling the pain by recognizing it. Remind
us of the beauty and necessity in our tears. Bring into focus our
child selves that wailed without shame. Remind us that our need is
not a nuisance. We've grown calloused from the overwhelming
helplessness of mass information. Call us back into a wholeness and
nuance that honor the dignity of the world with mourning. Soften
our hearts to tragedy, even our own. Bring us into proximity with
the wisely vulnerable, that they may teach us true courage. And
give us aids in our anguish, to journey with us in and out of sorrow.
Grant us ears to hear our own grief, and to welcome it into our body
as a friend once lost, found again. *Amen.*

FOR GRIEVING

God who knows sorrow,
We have nowhere to hide from this void. Thank you for being a
God who is moved to tears by death. For in doing so, you remind us
that one can know healing is imminent and still make space to
grieve what is. We're reminded that hope and grief are not mutually exclusive. Help us hold the departed in our minds, in our bones;
help us hear their laugh echo, their voice hum across our skin. But
also keep us from idolizing them in their absence, purging our
memory of their flaws, cleansing them in death of all that made
them human. May our mourning look how it must from one moment to the next, free from guilt about how much sadness we can
muster. And as we meet grief in all its complexity, grant us a small

company capable of remaining with us in our loss, those who journey with us as we heal. Not so they can speak platitudes or try to drag our souls toward happiness, but so they can hold space for our pain. Cast out any timeline we've made for our own healing. Remind us that grief rests and wakes as she chooses but remains with us across time. Help us to hold our tears as sacred, never being too quick to wipe them away or keep them prisoner, knowing that our freedom is wrapped up in theirs. *May it be so.*

FOR THE EXPLOITATION OF NATURE/CREATION

God of the land that cries out,
We confess that we have failed this land. We have bowed down to the convenience of machines and taken pleasure in our overconsumption. Grant us courage to name the atrocities of climate degradation, even when it implicates our daily habits. Upheave the corporations and institutions that leech off the earth without concern for its survival. Remind us that the welfare of creation is bound to our own. We cannot flourish on a landscape of ash and smoke. More than that, help us to decenter humanity in the story of the cosmos. Even if our time here is to end, plant in us an unchanging desire for the shalom of the earth we leave behind. Until then, amplify those who cry out for the dignity of all nature. Open our eyes to the gifts of simplicity, of creativity in energy sourcing, of building lives mindful of our impact, and of thinking not just about our days ahead, but generations to come. Show us, too, that our mourning is not just about how we treat creation, but the loss we face in failing to listen to it. For what elder have we older than the clouds, or the tides, or the wind in the leaves? May we grieve what has already been lost, and may we be granted time to heal what's been marred. *Amen.*

FOR BOUNDARIES IN OUR EMPATHY

God of shared tears,
This is too much to hold. Our bodies cannot take it. Release us from

the underlying guilt that we are not doing enough, crying enough, working hard enough. Sometimes it is easier to cry for another than for ourselves. Help us encounter our own emotions with the same attunement we possess for others. Develop our discernment for when our experience of the pain of others is good, and when it is an exercise in self-escape or saviorism. We confess that too often we give our attention only to receive attention. We perform empathy to feel a part of something. Protect us from the commodification of our shared lament. In all our efforts toward emotional solidarity, help us to truly center those who are hurting, and decenter the forces of whiteness that would leverage tragedy for profit. Expose how public performances of lament only serve to mask the detached morality of the most privileged. If we weep with the suffering, may their cries always ring louder. If we feel anything at all, make it honest. *Amen.*

FOR THOSE GRIEVING GLOBAL TERRORS

God who is moved to tears,
We have become desensitized to the cries of our neighbor. We confess that the trauma and terror of the world roll off us like oil. Help us to never become so familiar with pain that we grow disinterested in collective liberation. But keep us from that obsessive attunement which is prone toward savior complexes and feigned allyship. Lead us into a kind of solidarity that reminds us that in pausing to bear witness to suffering, we do not center ourselves as the rescuer. We do not become the voice. Free us from the responsibility to understand every tragedy at once. Help us to discern our capacity for solidarity, for lament. Help us to learn when to stand and when to rest and allow others to do so—remembering that our activism is shared among a collective. We don't have to hold it alone. *Amen.*

FOR THE INCARCERATED

God who breaks chains,
Remind us that we cannot speak of spiritual liberation without contending with the very real conditions of the jailed and imprisoned. We recognize how easy it is to ignore those behind bars. We have placed them strategically out of sight, where we can feign ignorance and remain impartial to their suffering. Show us the power of justice aligned with compassion. Overthrow this present corrupt system, which is another permutation of slavery under the guise of justice. Expose how our laws and prison system are not a means of protection but for profit. Destroy those institutions and organizations that exploit Black bodies, and grant tangible relief to the incarcerated. Protect their will, their courage, and their hope, that they would remember always their humanity cannot be diminished by a country that wants to destroy them. May they wake and rise each day in renewed belief in their dignity and all that they are worthy of. Grant them access to literature, art, and resources that remind them of who they are. And expand our imaginations for what accountability and redemption might look like, never forgetting the hand that holds the gavel is often capable of far greater evil than the hand confined to chains. *Amen.*

Breathe

INHALE: How long, O God?
EXHALE: This is too much to hold.

INHALE: I am not okay.
EXHALE: God, with you I am safe.

INHALE: I don't have to hold every pain at once.
EXHALE: I can feel and not be consumed.

INHALE: I won't rush my grief.
EXHALE: These tears are sacred.

Confession

Tender God,
We confess that we have forgotten what it means to feel fully. We have demeaned sadness as a lesser emotion, wielding it against women who are attuned to their pain and the pain of the world in a way we all should be. We have not cared well for little boys whose weeping is mocked and dismissed, training men toward an emotional constriction that poisons us all. We have exalted toxic positivity over complicated emotions, often rushing toward quick solutions and trite words of consolation instead of pausing to truly let suffering speak. We have been threatened by the tears of another more than we have tried to behold them, centering our own inability to be present to pain. Forgive us, God. Have mercy on all who dare to weep, who listen and heed the cries of the world. Forgive those who have forgotten how to lament, and grant that our souls might be moved at last, protected from despair on the journey. *Amen.*

Forgiveness

Let your soul receive this rest: May the God of many sorrows behold your tears before rushing to wipe them away. May they protect your grief from those who have everything to gain from its erasure. And may they have mercy on you and cradle you as you dare cry out for comfort in your own time. *Amen.*

Benediction

Go in freedom, with tearstained cheeks and stability of heart. Feel deeply and honestly, without being consumed. And may God hold fast to you if the tide of despair strengthens its pull, that you could grieve with the gravity you deserve. *Amen.*

Contemplation

1. Was there a time when you were tempted to expedite grief? Where did you learn this practice?
2. Explore a memory of when you were an agent or a victim of toxic positivity. What was the underlying fear?
3. Explore a memory of a time when your pain was co-opted or diluted. What would you say now that you weren't safe to say in that time?
4. What is the relationship between lament and despair in your life? What signals help you sense when the former is mutating into the latter?
5. What ritual of grief is meaningful to you? Dream up a new ritual of lament that you can practice as you need.

1 1

FEAR

*When fear rushed in, I learned how to hear my heart rac-
ing, but refused to allow my feelings to sway me. That
resilience came from my family. It flowed through our
bloodline.* —CORETTA SCOTT KING

*What difference do it make if the thing you scared of is
real or not?* —TONI MORRISON

LETTER XI | TO THOSE WHO TREMBLE

It is 2:13 A.M. and I've awoken to the sound of coyotes killing something. They are interesting animals because they can sound entirely
different depending on the night—chirping, squealing, moaning.
Sometimes their howls sound human.

Once I'm awake it takes hours for me to fall asleep again. I'm not
afraid of the coyotes anymore; I've lived on this land for years. But
it's like the memory of being afraid awakens fears of all other kinds.
I start thinking about all these future scenarios, some plausible,
others certainly not. I script out conversations in my head and recite
them again and again with the slightest adjustments. *This is what
you'll say on the day your literary agent realizes she's made a mistake on you. This is how you'll beg or never beg. This is where you'll
hide when your neighbors with the MAGA flags and hunting rifles
come for you. This is how you'll board the windows. This is how you'll
fight. How you'll cry.* Many nights, I've buried my father.

More than most things, I'm afraid. When I say this, people always seem to want to assure me that it isn't the case. But we know.
Since I was little, I would always find a way to imagine the worst
possible versions of the future. Maybe on some level I've grown to

believe if I prepare for it, it will hurt less when it comes. But it makes for an agitated body and mind. When you always expect a demon around every corner, your most mundane moments still feel like a risk.

On the day my sister gave birth, I threw up for hours. I wasn't just afraid she would die; in my body, she was already dead. In preparing for the worst, I was living her death again and again by the hour. My chest pressed against itself, and my face was fire, and there I was waiting on the bathroom floor with my husband assuring me that she was going to be fine. Only this was not a promise he could make. Not in a country where maternal mortality rates for Black women are three times higher than for white women. Sometimes our fear is the most credible emotion we have access to. Sometimes we have everything to fear.

What do we do when our fears are in fact rational? When fear and wisdom are enmeshed? When we would be foolish *not* to fear? More often than we realize, fear is a protective intuition. It is what stops you from driving with no headlights on, from touching your hand to flame, from going outside to meet the coyotes. We don't have to demonize our fear to survive it. For this reason, I have an aversion to language of "conquering" our fears. We are not at war with ourselves; it is better to listen with compassion.

As a child, maybe you were told there is nothing to be afraid of. As adults, when we're most honest, I think we know we have everything to be afraid of. This world, which has been so unsafe to so many of us, cannot be trusted not to harm us again. This isn't pessimism, it's confession.

Still, to live in a constant state of fear will keep you from the rest you were meant for. They are near opposites, fear and rest. It is not likely that you'll relax those shoulders if somewhere within you feel the house is on fire. I want us to honor our fears without being tormented by them. Sacred intuition without restlessness.

This quote from James L. Farmer is at the front of my journal: "Courage, after all, is not being unafraid, but doing what needs to be done in spite of fear." The implication, of course, is that if you're not scared, it's not courage. If there is any bravery in me, it is in my refusal to let fear eclipse my imagination for anything other than pain. To maintain imagination for both the beautiful *and* the terrible is to marry prudence and hope. This is how you fall asleep to howling.

I cannot promise you everything will be okay. But breathe. Listen. You are no coward. You are making it best you can in a land of many haunts. I'll stay awake with you, just like this, until you're ready to close your eyes. Breathe. Whatever is to come, or never comes, we'll take turns keeping watch.

From the dark,
C

A Litany for Survival

by Audre Lorde

For those of us who live at the shoreline
standing upon the constant edges of decision
crucial and alone
for those of us who cannot indulge
the passing dreams of choice
who love in doorways coming and going
in the hours between dawns
looking inward and outward
at once before and after
seeking a now that can breed
futures
like bread in our children's mouths
so their dreams will not reflect
the death of ours;

For those of us
who were imprinted with fear
like a faint line in the center of our foreheads
learning to be afraid with our mother's milk
for by this weapon
this illusion of some safety to be found
the heavy-footed hoped to silence us
For all of us
this instant and this triumph
We were never meant to survive.

And when the sun rises we are afraid
it might not remain
when the sun sets we are afraid

it might not rise in the morning
when our stomachs are full we are afraid
of indigestion
when our stomachs are empty we are afraid
we may never eat again
when we are loved we are afraid
love will vanish
when we are alone we are afraid
love will never return
and when we speak we are afraid
our words will not be heard
nor welcomed
but when we are silent
we are still afraid

So it is better to speak
remembering
we were never meant to survive.

Prayers

FOR WHEN COURAGE FEELS FAR FROM YOU

God of those who tremble,
Courage can feel foolish when we've seen the world in all its terror.
But, protect us from life lived in perpetual vigilance. Keep fear from
monopolizing our relationships, our desires, our motivations, so that
we can act without rehearsing the worst of our imaginations. Help
us meet our fear with kindness and mercy. There are times when we
feel small and exhausted. Harness our courage. Grant us contentment in our limits, and community in our battles. Send others who
tremble alongside us, who will speak truth with calmness. Show us
we need not be giants if we have good friends. And lead us beside
still waters. The space is thin between bravery and rest. Remind us
that fear is as bodily as any emotion. Slow our breath, ground our
attention. Lie still with us as courage finds us. *May it be so.*

FOR THOSE WHOSE ANXIETY IS A MENACE

God of sleepless nights,
How can we rest when fear has made a home in us? Our bodies are
riddled with anxiety, so we eat, and look at screens, and lash out,
and do a thousand unhelpful things to placate, if only for a moment, the tension rising in us. We have known an elusive anxiety—
a fear that cannot be placed or rationalized. We have been tormented by our own imaginations. Protect us from being alienated
by our fear and draw us into communities of patience and understanding. Steady us in your arms, God. That your presence with us
would be a mother's tenderness. That we would be rocked and
swayed, but that it would be the kind of rocking that comforts us in
the arms of our maker and sustainer. Let us breathe deep, keeping
rhythm with the chest of God. *Amen.*

FOR THOSE WHO DOOMSCROLL

Still God,
We confess we are addicted to pessimism. Although we rarely name it as such, so much of our attention is devoted to negativity. Show us how we use technology to soothe and stir the aches in us. Keep us from turning control over to our anxiety, that it would no longer feed itself with news of tragedy and impending disaster. It is easy to become lost, buried in the quicksand of digital catastrophe. Draw our attention upward. Guide us to look away habitually; and not just away, but up at the sky, the grass, the table. Guide us inward as well. Acquaint us with goodness again. In the world, and in ourselves. Let us follow the children, freed from the grip of seriousness. Renew our playfulness. Lead us into wise rhythms of engagement, retreating to rest and breathe. Remind us that there is much the world needs, including our attention to atrocity—but if we watch the world burn for long enough, the fire will become our only reality. *Amen.*

FOR THE UNKNOWN

God of shadows,
Our fear of the unknown keeps us from moving at all. Help us not to know. Protect our minds when anxious thoughts about the future refuse to leave us alone. Deepen our breath. Bring us into communities who can be trusted when they tell us we are safe. Comfort us when our minds become frenzied trying to determine what we cannot possibly know. When questions of what is to come or who will stay with us haunt us, make us kind with our own self-talk, tender to our bodies, loving with all we do have control over. When no amount of courage can diminish fear's power over us, remind us that we too have power as we rise to meet it. Provide a way to peace. We will not fear the dark. *Ase.*

FOR THE WALK HOME AT NIGHT

God of dimly lit streets,
Embolden us to tell the truth about a society that has not only stood by predators but worshipped them. Validate the marginalized, who know the true risk of putting our fate in the hands of men. Keep us from being drowned out by the sadistic social power that lays blame at the feet of the vulnerable. Release us from shame and strengthen our resolve against the pitiful weakness of abuse. We are grateful to those who have told their stories. Grant rest to the traumatized, and sew solidarity into the lives of those who listen. Renew our trust in ourselves, our intuition, our capacity to see through masks and believe one another. Unfold the power of women to heal and tear down forces of abuse and exploitation. May we reclaim everything they thought themselves capable of stealing. *Amen.*

FOR WHEN YOU NEED TO RUN AND HIDE

Wise God,
Break the false belief in us that all fear is the enemy. When danger in the world comes for us, make trepidation our ally. Focus our fear on the real. Free us from the shame heaped on victims, and reveal the manipulation of the oppressors who claim our worry is irrational. Remind us that fear and wisdom have a sacred relationship, developing our intuition as a spiritual gift. Show us how to fear for others out of love. Replace the derision of our child fears with tenderness, leading us into memory that honors the wise trembling of our youth. Do not let fear keep us in perpetual flight, but let it usher us into community, drawing us into the safe embrace of others. *Amen.*

FOR COMING OUT

Queer God,
We know who we are. And we thank you for a self-knowledge that is at once terrifying and liberating. Stay near as we continue to

share that knowledge with others. From youth, a special kind of fear has haunted our every interaction. We have been intimidated and alienated by words, spoken and unspoken, from those who were oblivious to the truth of us. We have done what we must to survive. Alleviate any guilt we may carry for what remains hidden. Remind us that our dignity cannot be extinguished, even by rejection. As we grieve the death of so many queer people, keep us from being overcome by powerlessness, or the fear that halts liberation. As we grieve the unique fear that stalks the lives of Black trans women, may we become honest about their erasure within our own communities. Just as you contain multitudes, teach us to not just *name* our particularities, but relentlessly pursue safety for all who tremble. And may we welcome those who are still hidden within our sacred number. May we shelter them, tend to them, and fight for them as we continue the path toward the truth of us. *Amen.*

Breathe

INHALE: I will not be silenced by fear.
EXHALE: A quivering voice is still sacred.

INHALE: God, my soul trembles.
EXHALE: Steady me in your arms.

INHALE: I will meet this fear with rest.
EXHALE: God, steady me in your arms.

Confession

Mother God,
We are terrified. So many different fears have been watered and grown in us that there are days when it feels like we are more afraid than human. We confess that we have let fear grow louder than our own voice. We have let fear grow louder than the voices of those who love us. Those fears that are healthy, we have alienated and demonized, favoring the theater of bravery over the true practice of

it. We've escalated fear in some in order to control them, and dismissed the fears of others in order to feel superior to them. Steady us and have mercy on us, that we would know courage. *Amen.*

Forgiveness

Let your soul receive this rest: The God who wakes to comfort her child in the night rises for you. Feel her cradle you and comfort you, never punishing you for your dread but meeting it with tenderness and understanding. Let her free you from those worries that seek to control you, and remain with you in any fear that is meant to protect you. Through this forgiveness, be guided into rest, that you would fall asleep in safe places and wake renewed. *Amen.*

Benediction

May you live each day with sacred intuition to the terrors of this world. But may you never be swallowed by them. May you find peace as you let the divine guide you into inner rest in the face of all that might destroy you. May you tremble, but never alone. *Amen.*

Contemplation

1. What fears tend to dictate how you exist in the world? Can you pinpoint their origin?
2. What do you believe about the relationship between fear and weakness? How did you learn this? Explore a story.
3. How does fear change your communication?
4. We often try to defuse fear by convincing one another that there is no reason to be afraid. Is this true for the fears you have? How do you wish your fear was held by others?

1 2

RAGE

If abandoned rage asks, Who should answer for this?
Say, the very blood of our lives eats composure up.
—CLAUDIA RANKINE

My rage intensifies because I am not a victim. It burns in
my psyche with an intensity that creates clarity. It is a
constructive healing rage.... [It is] a way for us to learn
to see clearly
—BELL HOOKS

LETTER XII | TO LUNGS THAT HOLD MORE THAN AIR

I'll begin with honesty. When someone comments that my father is
a deadbeat on a Black Liturgies post about Juneteenth, it's the
sound of my own laughter that startles me. And I laugh again when
I show my husband before tossing a bowl in the sink with a little
more force than is necessary. We block them, and I pretend I won't
think about it at the most random times for the rest of the day.

I haven't attuned to my own anger in any meaningful way in
over a year. I haven't *allowed myself* to feel angry. And on the rare
occasion I've felt it, I quickly disguise it as some other more palat-
able emotional expression. I'm not angry, I'm laughing. There are
times when this is necessary to my own survival. But nearly as often,
this is one of many symptoms of distrust in me. Or maybe it's myself that I'm afraid of.

I'm scared to tell you to embrace your anger, because I don't
know what's been done to you. It seems irresponsible to advocate for
the release of any rage without knowing the stories your rage contains. We don't need centuries of patriarchal white supremacy to
tell us not all anger is safe. Perhaps it wasn't safe in your home. Or

your school. Or on the walk to your car at night. The anger of some has long been used as a tool to dominate others.

For this reason, many of us have learned to alienate our anger from our other emotional experiences. Happiness and sadness and even fear are met with tenderness, understanding; they are permitted to speak without constant interior scrutiny. But anger we require to use the back door—to come and go quietly without drawing too much attention to itself. And on the occasion it takes a seat at the table—when we yell or curse or dare to grimace—we rush to assure ourselves that this is not who we are. That we are "better than this." This alienation will always reward the tyrant, never the terrorized. The same cultural rhetoric that tells you your anger is mean or "uncivilized" is the spawn of those who strung up our ancestors from trees and beat them bloody with batons. And sold them. And burned them. The reason whiteness is so terrified of our anger is because it only contains memory of (and imagination for) how its own anger has been practiced in the world.

But as Audre Lorde reminds us in "The Uses of Anger," "It is not the anger of Black women which is dripping down over this globe like a diseased liquid. It is not my anger that launches rockets, spends over sixty thousand dollars a second on missiles and other agents of war and death, slaughters children in cities, stockpiles nerve gas and chemical bombs, sodomizes our daughters and our earth. It is not the anger of Black women which corrodes into blind, dehumanizing power, bent upon the annihilation of us all."

Years ago, when I was living alone in Philly and had no friends to spend New Year's Eve with, I came up with a list of about twelve rituals to honor the passage of time. Running with my eyes closed for twenty seconds. Writing a letter to my next-year self. Drawing my face in the dark. The first year, I performed most of these rituals alone. But with every year that passed, I would add to my number, slowly inviting others. Until one year I looked up and there were about ten of us outside at midnight cracking a watermelon open against the ground and eating the pieces with juice dripping down our frozen arms.

There are other rituals, but one of them in particular offers a unique kind of catharsis.

There we stand—staggered and shivering in the darkness next to the barn. The children among us giggle nervously, tucking themselves into the warmth of their father. Someone glances at their watch and counts us down. *Three*—and we squint at each other, eyes darting from face to face. *Two*—and we're inhaling with a singular mouth, letting our bellies descend beneath us. *One*—and we're screaming. One long and aching and terrible scream. Some of us run out of breath sooner than the others. We gasp for air and let out a second howl—fists clenched, veins bulging. And another. And another. Some of us barely know each other, but in the absurdity of this act, we're known. Even the children aren't giggling anymore; they are young, but they are old enough to know that they have something to scream for. And together in the dark, we allow our anger to take up the space it is often denied the other days of the year. It's a reclamation practice.

Without fail, it seems as if each year there are one or two newcomers to whom we have to explain the rituals. The 11:00 P.M. scream yields the most resistance. And as much as we prepare them, they are always surprised to find that when we say scream, it is precisely what we mean. Full sound, lungs gasping, in-the-body kind of scream. It is a vulnerable thing to be known in this way. So, the newcomer will begin restrained, eyes flitting around waiting to see how willing everyone else is to be known. And then by the second scream, there is a shift. The insecurity in them begins to quiet, and they realize that no one cares about how squeaky or raspy or scared or angry they sound. This ritual—this collective demonstration of anger—is safe. And in its own way, liberating.

The group dynamic always shifts after 11:00 P.M. We walk back to the house and people begin to move just a little bit closer to one another. By the time we return to the light, no one is shivering anymore.

You were not meant to live life constricted. The oppressors of this world have told you to play nice, be civil. They tell you to control yourself. But by this, they only mean they want you easy to be controlled. Don't be mistaken, your anger doesn't have to look like that of those who seek to destroy you. There is an anger that affirms dignity instead of degrading it.

For humanity, for those you love, and for yourself—you can rage. You can shout in the dark for things you don't even have the words for. Your anger is sacred, a protector of goodness in a menacing world. Do not cage it up, letting it chew through you from the inside out. Send the teeth where they're meant to go.

Unapologetically,

C

Mount Carmel

And fuck everyone who didn't
Say a word when
They got him.
We never were meant to know that
blood pools to black
not red.
You who said
be civil
as you hosed down
the sidewalk.
You who said
It takes time
as you washed the smirk from your mouth.
And peace smells
Toxic on your tongue and
Every acid has its use.

When the prophet called
The fire down
I heard no apology;
The flame was a mirror.

Elijah, 23 and loved cats.
His hands—loving—caressed
And kneaded
the knots in our shoulders.
He could've healed you

But you shot him up with ketamine and watched him call you
beautiful.

You watched him writhe
now watch
as it's your own flesh
that's eaten
those tightened muscles quivering
beneath you
I don't believe a word
Because you didn't believe him
you exposed
you nasty
you corroded miserable thing.

Prayers

FOR THOSE WHO ARE FAR FROM THEIR ANGER

God who burns within,
We have buried our anger in commands that you never gave it.
We've judged it as evil, willfully ignoring that our rage refracts a
Maker who demonstrated an emotional anger in the prophets and
an embodied anger on the day you overturned tables of injustice.
We have exalted being nice and calm as a pinnacle of character,
repressing that which stirs our souls so deeply we must shout. So
many have wielded language of civility against the oppressed in
attempts to mitigate their own discomfort and guilt. For, to face the
depths of their anger is to be implicated in the systems and situations that have birthed it. Release us from the kind of niceness that
only serves and protects the oppressor. And help us to also be gentle
with the trauma that may have alienated us from the truth of what
we feel. Awaken our collective rage in defense of dignity in the
world. Provide safe friends to hear and hone the private emotions
that have been silenced for so long. Together, we will no longer
abandon ourselves. Make us people of holy fury. *Ase.*

FOR BLACK WOMEN

Liberating God,
We are exhausted from living within the narrow quarters that the
world has constructed for us. Our societies fail to recognize the full
spectrum of human emotions because they fail to recognize our
humanity itself. For too long we have been villainized for our rage,
when we have had to be wiser, more strategic, and more accommo-
dating than any other population on earth. Keep us from surrender-
ing our anger out of fear of being reduced to it. We deserve better
than that. Ground us in the same fire that protected the women

who came before us. Grant us a sacred company that does not require our anger to be polished or contained in order for us not to be destroyed. Give us friends who aren't threatened when we name a thing for what it is and don't shrink back. Let our rage pass down to our daughters, that they would never settle for anything less than dignity. And let our anger be a beacon to the rest of the world, whose attunement to their own rage is so atrophied that all they can do is demonize ours. In us, may they glimpse an emotional truth-telling that heals. Make ours a beautiful rage. *Ase.*

FOR BLACK PEOPLE WHO HAD TO SMILE THROUGH IT

God who knows the cost,
These grins are heavy. But there are times when we cannot afford to shed them safely. Time and time again we have had to temper our anger, cool down, step away, or smile as injustice unfolds. Redeem these moments of restraint in the face of indignity. Heal the emotional wounds from the accusation and restriction whiteness has placed over our feelings, as it is unable to reckon with its own deformed emotional life. Undo the epigenetic consequences of emotional constriction. Release us from feeling shame toward the grins that have kept us alive, and remind us that the moral liability for our oppression is on whiteness. As we continue on the path of liberation, let us scream. Let smile become scowl. Let our rage boil enough to melt chains themselves, in holy remembrance of the masks our ancestors were forced to wear. Give us our faces back. *Ase.*

FOR TEMPERS

God who regulates,
We confess that we have let our anger loose on those we hate and those we love. Protect our relationships with those we've harmed. There are times when our fear of losing someone is so large in us, we do terrible things to push them away before they can leave.

There are times when our anger is a mask for fear, triggered by the memory of harm, abuse, or neglect. Our rage deserves better than the miserable hole we've placed it in. Incline our ears toward every rash or violent choice, listening for the sound of past pain or buried conflict. Direct our anger not toward annihilation but the pursuit of justice and care, that it would serve as a sanctifying presence in our lives. Something that draws us into deeper connection instead of alienating us from it. Help us be careful with our bodies in our outbursts, the damage we can do to them, and the pain they can inflict. Keep us from viewing our bodies as weapons and let us reclaim them in their beauty and softness. Train us how to regulate ourselves in a dysregulated world, that we would pause, breathe, never letting our anger colonize our minds. That we would pause, breathe, knowing anger can live here—a sacred fire keeping us warm without burning us to the ground. *Amen.*

FOR A WORLD WHERE CHILDREN HAVE TO PRACTICE HIDING UNDER THEIR DESKS

Divine Protector,
Our world is plagued with unimaginable evil that destroys the most innocent among us. Make our anger loud. Never let us become comfortable with hearing that children have been sacrificed on the altars of our own distorted political agendas. Disrupt the politicization of mass murder and hold the enablers of school shootings to account. Make way for the emotional healing of victims, families, and all those who have been conditioned to expect horror. Cultivate communities who can untangle the distorted reality that white supremacy has instilled in its youth; a distortion that says it's normal to brace for death so young, to know which desk to hide under. Guard the minds and hearts of children for whom safety is foreign, and remind us that raising children is a communal responsibility. Their lives depend on not just our grief, but a righteous rage that leads to action. When we say "never again," may we mean it. *Amen.*

Breathe

INHALE: There is space for my anger.
EXHALE: My pain won't be dismissed.

INHALE: I will not grow numb.
EXHALE: There is beauty in anger.

INHALE: My truth-telling is a gift.
EXHALE: I am free to say so.

Confession

God of the prophets,
We confess that we have demonized anger, confining it to an interior prison instead of granting it time and space to be free, just like any other piece of our selfhood. We have not acted in defense of those who've needed it. We have let fear of how we might be perceived keep us from the truth-telling that others are worthy of, that we are worthy of. We have ignored anger in our bodies, disguising it with whichever mask feels good to us. We have valued the comfort of the wounder over the dignity of the wounded. Have mercy on us for all that suppression has stolen from us. Forgive us our emotional numbness, and grant us access to safe rage, collective rage, a rage that liberates. *Amen.*

Forgiveness

Let your soul receive this rest: The God who flipped the tables of greed and exclusion in the temple forgives us for holding our anger captive. The divine remains in our bodies as we destroy the tables of injustice still standing today. May God sharpen our tongues, that we would speak with precision and emotion. With them, we are kept from punishing ourselves for all the times we were silenced in the past. With them, we open our mouths now for all that we've lost.

Benediction

Awake, awake, oh sleeper. Be reminded that the world deserves so much more than apathy in the presence of injustice. Go with anger, not as enemy but as guardian. A sacred protector in a world of so much hatred, reminding us we deserve to be protected. We breathe, we feel. And we befriend our anger as if the liberation of the world depends on it. *May it be so.*

Contemplation

1. What was your family of origin's relationship to anger? Who did it manifest in, and in what ways?
2. What is your relationship to anger in this season? In what ways are you or aren't you prone to suppression?
3. Explore different instinctive feelings about individual rage versus collective rage. Does either feel more appropriate or inappropriate to you? Why do you think that is?
4. Where have you seen rage practiced well? What made it a healthy demonstration of anger?
5. Which emotions do you disguise your anger with? How did you learn to do this?
6. Travel into a memory when someone demonized your anger. Imagine what you would do or say today.

13

SECRETS

*There are some words that once spoken will split the world
in two. There would be the life before you breathed them
and then the altered life after they'd been said. They take
a long time to find, words like that. They make you hesi-
tate. Choose with care.* —ANDREA LEVY

If you can't be free, be a mystery. —RITA DOVE

LETTER XIII | TO THE ONES WHO CAN KEEP A SECRET

In writing to you about secrets, I feel a certain pressure to disclose
one myself. I've waited to write this letter hoping one would occur
to me that didn't feel too costly, but wouldn't appear to you to have
been told without cost. I want to tell you something that means
something. I want to tell you something that means absolutely
nothing.

I'm a private person. Not everyone perceives this of me, and I
don't know how to tell them that if I appear vulnerable to them, it
is only because I have tried to construct the illusion of vulnerability
so as to avoid sharing what I have no interest in sharing.

I don't just have secrets; I have an entire note on my laptop (written in abbreviations) that outlines what stories I've told, what I
have chosen to keep a secret, what I have shared with the greater
public, and what I never will. I don't just have secrets; I live by
them.

When I was little, I would hide my things in odd places and I
would detail in my journal exactly how I had placed them, just to
determine if anyone had moved them while I was gone. The ob-
jects were of no value; I just wanted to know if my sister could be

trusted. It was a test. And it is because she passed these countless tests that I will confess something to her now. This one is not for you; it's for her, because this letter will likely never make it to her:

When you asked me if I burned a hole in your dress—the blue and purple one with the diagonal lines down the side— and I told you "no" and made you feel dumb for thinking I would ever have access to matches, I was lying. I wasn't trying to burn your dress, I was trying to burn the edges of my diary so it looked like some old and important artifact. And it wasn't matches, but Dad's lighter, and I'm lying again because maybe it started that way: me, huddled in a closet with a stolen lighter and my diary. But then I did see your dress. You know the one, tight enough to remind everyone how much thinner you were than me. It was sleeveless and reminded me of the time I was told I couldn't wear shirts that showed my big arms like that. That I needed to dress for my body. Anyway, I saw the dress and I lit it up. It took more time than you would think to get a hole burnt through. And if I made you feel stupid for asking, it is only because I felt stupid for doing it. And ugly. But I couldn't afford for you to know I felt ugly. So, the hole. And the secret. Maybe you already knew.

I was a secretive child. In a family of enchanting but imposing extroverts, I thirsted for solitude. But as it was sparse to come by, secrets became a form of solitude no one could take from me. For better or for worse. If you yourself can't be hidden, at least some indirect piece of you can.

Ocean Vuong wrote, "To be gorgeous, you must first be seen, but to be seen allows you to be hunted." This is where I tell you I was sexually abused as a child. Which is to say, I was being hunted. I couldn't afford to be seen. I've always heard secrets make you sick. But some secrets save your life. Not everyone can be trusted to find you without destroying you.

Maybe I had so many secrets because it felt like sharing any of them might open the door and send the biggest one creeping out to ruin me. There was little trust left in me; I won't criticize myself for this.

But with every year that passes, I have slowly rebuilt the trust that was stolen from me. I have a few friends who go to no minor lengths to know me. I let them hold my stories. I do the same for them. They don't force or guilt me into disclosure; it's an invitation. I tell you this because the secrets you are too terrified to utter one year, you might several years later find yourself discussing over cold leftovers while the TV hums in the background.

I will not demonize your hidden parts, just as I cannot promise you that they will be met with tenderness and care once you bring them out of hiding. But I can say, no one should be alone for too long. There are secrets that feel like beauty and those that feel like bondage. Don't burn holes into yourself.

I won't blame you if you never say it out loud. Who am I to un-latch the door? But I can wait with you, hide with you for as long as you need. Right here. You don't have to say a word.

From hiding,
C

Confessional

We bought speakers to make us feel something, but I'm sensitive to noise so we can only use them if one of us is bracing their thumb against the volume button.

There we sit—in sonic limbo—you turning up for dialogue and down for the sound effects, thumb always hovering.

But if we let our guards down, if we ever get to thinking I am any braver than I never was—a crash, or a clap, and there are my shoulders wrapped around my neck, there my sternum pressing into my beating heart, and I don't recover well because it's the door slamming and it's the crash of dirty ceramic against the sink, and I'm somewhere else altogether and
don't ask me to tell you why I'm screaming.

A month ago, I told my therapist about our new speakers, how I secretly poured a glass of gin over them so I would stop yelling at you like you'd done something unforgivable. I told her how I'm jumping at everything including the sound of your voice. She told me noise sensitivity is a trauma response and when she says the word *anxiety,* I barely hear her. If I didn't mention it, it's only because I love you. If I didn't help you carry the fried black boxes tangled in wire, it's only because people shouldn't hold their own tombs.

Prayers

FOR FAMILY SECRETS

God of what whispers through our blood,
We have inherited secrets that never were meant to belong to us.
Explicitly or implicitly, we have learned to protect family members
with a silence that now haunts us. Teach us what are secrets of tenderness and intimacy, and what are secrets that isolate us from anyone who could dare to comfort us or help us. Release us from the
pressure to protect blood at all costs, especially when our own blood
and bone refuses to protect us. Help us to know what of our family
story is or isn't for those outside the walls. And alleviate any guilt
we may feel in exposing what has long been hidden, that we would
know that those who came before us ached for the liberation that
we ourselves are grabbing hold of. Remind us that sometimes to
open the front door to others is to save the very people who are
trapped inside. And just as we've inherited the lock, so too have we
inherited the key. *Amen.*

FOR KEEPING SOMEONE ELSE'S SECRET

Trusted One,
I don't know what to do with the secret I've been trusted to carry. It's
a weight that I am terrified to betray, and terrified not to. What will
become of us? Guide me as I make sense of what integrity looks like
in this. Help me to ask wise questions and speak as honestly as I can
while protecting those who need to be protected. Place before me
many possibilities for how to hold this secret, that I would not be
confined to an oversimplification of right and wrong, and can move
with both compassion and caution. Help me to care for this person
well, never infantilizing them or stripping them of their own agency,
but always being clear with them about what of the secret I can or
cannot keep hidden. Let us perceive of any present and ongoing

threats, and be with us as we rise to protect and defend against them. And when it's safe and ethical to do so, may you grant me the wisdom and stability of heart to do what needs to be done to protect the most vulnerable involved. I know what can be lost. Show me how to carry the secret with compassion for both the hurting and myself. God, stay near. Bring help. Bring healing. *Amen.*

FOR HEALTHY VULNERABILITY

God of the untold,
We are raw. Many times, we have had our pain used as a means to make other people feel like they have achieved some kind of intimacy. Reveal these people as vultures of emotion and reveal these moments as a feeding ground for those who are emptied of their own stories. Protect us from fleeting sentimentality and shallow displays of vulnerability. We have grown wary of communal spaces that ask us to bare ourselves for their sake, without ever becoming thoughtful about how they will care for and love us in the midst of our rawness. Liberate us from the lie that vulnerability is the only form of relational closeness. Remind us that some stories aren't meant for everyone and that is good and okay. And in the presence of those who are more interested in using us to rouse emotion in their emptiness, help us to choose ourselves—our wholeness; that we would practice a sacred withholding that mirrors the mysteries of the one who made us. *May it be so.*

FOR THE MASKS THAT GNAW AT YOU

God of every veil,
Some days we find ourselves tormented by our secrets. Our worst choices, our every action or failure to act, taunt us from the past. We silently critique ourselves, and we bar others from entering and holding us in the dark corridors of our own hearts. Grant us a communal and self-compassion that releases us from the fear of being known. Help us toward a forgiveness that isn't too quick or too slow,

but that lives relentlessly at the site of our own truth-telling, remorse, and repair. And as you release us from our guilt, guide us toward a self-forgiveness that allows us to operate not out of blame or terror, but out of a deep sense of belonging and love. May we entrust ourselves to those capable of seeing us unveiled—those who won't discard or devalue us for the secret, but who will approach our true faces and remind us of our dignity. We are exhausted from hiding. We are parched for some semblance of truth on our tongue. Guide us to clear waters, that we might live. *Amen.*

FOR THOSE WHO FEEL ASHAMED

God our seamstress,

Call us out of our shame. We are curled up inside ourselves, afraid to be seen because we cannot bear the sight of our own faces. But this is agony. Remind us what we were meant for. When Adam and Eve hid from you and covered their bodies out of shame, you were the God who knelt down in the dirt to make them clothing. Help us to remember that it is not your character to humiliate, but to do whatever you can so that we might come out of our hiding and stand in the presence of one another again. Free us from the secret things we speak over ourselves—words of self-hatred and disgust. Guide us toward a self-understanding that heals, and release us from the ugly wanderings of mind and spirit that pull us back into hiding. Remind us that shame is a liar. We will not give our chains a voice. *Amen.*

Breathe

INHALE: I can protect my story.
EXHALE: I don't owe them all of me.

INHALE: This secret is a prison.
EXHALE: I can open the door.

INHALE: I won't hide from myself.
EXHALE: God is not the sound of shame.

Confession

Secret God,

We confess we have cultivated habits of distrust and dishonesty. We have not honored the stories that have been shared with us, often centering ourselves and our own hunger for emotional theater and false intimacy over the hurting. We have failed to offer care to those who have bared themselves to us, leaving them emotionally spent and alone. We have kept secrets in the interest of protecting the powerful, and we have told secrets in a way that erodes trust between us and those we love. We have shamed and we have been shamed. Forgive us. Have mercy on us and be with us in our hiding, that we would reclaim a discerning posture toward the hidden things and question any exposure that leaves us more raw than real. *Amen.*

Forgiveness

Let your soul receive this rest: The God of deep mystery will teach you the beauty and terror of what is hidden. Receive forgiveness for all your attempts at exposing what should remain secret, and all your attempts to hold alone that which deserves to be held by another. Feel divine mercy over you, protecting you as you endure the cost of what is hidden. Be comforted as you try to do your best in a world that cannot always be trusted to hold the untold parts of your story. And find compassion for yourself as you choose to tell or not tell. However close you allow others to get, the divine remains near. *Amen.*

Benediction

Go in compassion, to become more and more honest with yourself as you protect your story in the way that you need to. Go in honor, liberated from the shame that thrives in hidden places, and with renewed love and respect for the face encountered in the mirror. *Amen.*

Contemplation

1. Are you more prone to oversharing or withholding? Why do you think this is?

2. How do you determine what of your story can be held safely by someone, and what can remain hidden?

3. What is a secret in your life that you need to remain hidden for now? How does it feel when you imagine sharing it with someone you trust? How does it feel speaking it aloud to yourself?

4. What family secrets have you been led to protect? What has the cost been?

5. What fears are your family secrets grounded in? What would be at stake if the truth came to light?

14

POWER

It's not about supplication, it's about power. It's not about asking, it's about demanding. It's not about convincing those who are currently in power, it's about changing the very face of power itself.

—KIMBERLÉ WILLIAMS CRENSHAW

One of the greatest problems of history is that the concepts of love and power are usually contrasted as polar opposites.... What is needed is a realization that power without love is reckless and abusive and that love without power is sentimental and anemic.

—MARTIN LUTHER KING, JR.

LETTER XIV | TO THE ONES
IN STEP WITH CHILDREN

When ten thousand Black people marched down Fifth Avenue in the heat of July, it was the children, all in white, who led them. Then the women. Then all others. There were no songs or chants, no megaphones. Just the sound of them—their steps, their breath, the soft vibrations of muffled drums holding together their footsteps. It would come to be known as the Silent Parade. 1917—shortly following the East St. Louis Race Riot, in which a crowd of white residents shot, hanged, and burned hundreds of Black people and their homes. White mobs, terrible and inhumane in their power, led bloody slaughters all over the country that summer. In response, one of the first protests of its kind was formed.

I tell you they were led by the children because I want you to ask yourself what it means to meet the evils of white power with a power that looks nothing like them. There is something unquestionably strange—tender and beautiful strangeness—in Black organizers deciding that they would be led by the young. That they would believe that these children had just as much power to protest as they did. And I think about how it is more than mere symbol that every adult in the crowd would have had to submit themselves to the pace of hundreds of tiny child footsteps. A redistribution of power in the body.

I tell you they were silent because what if good power requires solemn creativity? Their silence, I'm sure, was in stark contrast to the taunts and vitriol aimed toward them by white people. It was a way to say, our power doesn't look like your power. Chins high, keeping step with children; our power doesn't look like your power. I don't mean to imply that strength must always be silent, but I do believe it must be a product of collective dreaming. Silence was subversive. There are times when our song is equally so. Our task is to expand our imaginations for what power looks like.

How do we decide the face of power? Whom and what are we most inclined to follow? Scholar Isabel Wilkerson wrote, "The right kind of leader can inspire a symbiotic connection that supplants logic. The susceptible group sees itself in the narcissistic leader, becomes one with the leader, sees his fortunes and his fate as their own. 'The greater the leader,' Fromm wrote, 'the greater the follower. . . . The narcissism of the leader who is convinced of his greatness, and who has no doubts, is precisely what attracts the narcissism of those who submit to him.'" This is what I know: I cannot afford to spend all my energies trying to locate the humanity of those who wish to destroy me. I leave that interior quest to them, and the desperate souls who follow them. What humanity has deteriorated in the leader, so too has deteriorated in the followers.

In our government, in our educational institutions, in our courts, and on the doctor's table, we see the face of the tyrant. It grins as it bans Black books in schools, and scowls when we love who we love. A power so malformed, so malnourished of any kind of humanity that there is no way forward but to eradicate the moral cancer and rebuild under the leadership and imagination of the historically excluded.

From Assata Shakur: "Nobody in the world, nobody in history, has ever gotten their freedom by appealing to the moral sense of the people who were oppressing them." Maybe you've known what it means to exist under the thumb of someone who never wanted you to survive. Maybe you've sat in rooms where people speak right through you. Walked down streets at night with keys digging into knuckles. Worked eighty hours just to not be able to afford your medication. I know helplessness; it convinces you of all kinds of things. But not all power is synonymous with domination, and not all freedom means free from all constraint. If control over your present circumstances has been kept from you, there is still a power in you that cannot be easily withheld.

You are the descendant of a mystical force, subversive power. You, who are still here—breathing, dreaming. Do not exhaust yourself trying to prove your humanity to those who have no interest in remaining human themselves. Do not petition for what's written in your bones. Claim it, an interior and creative power. As we wait for the tyrants of this world to be cast out at last. As we wait for compassion and care to take her seat and push the world back on its axis.

Resisting with you,

C

Appetite

When the big man flipped
The ladybug on its back
It was only to keep it from flying
At his heavy head

And when the ladybug found her legs again
He pinched her up
And crunched her flat between
Two fingers

Don't make me
do this
And he already had

When the little boy grabbed
The big man's hand
It was only to rub it against
his soft cheek

And when he caught
A whiff of death on the same
hands that carry him to bed
He asked him how it felt
To kill a thing with wings

Prayers

FOR GLOBAL POWERS AND OUR HABITS OF EXCLUSION

Just God,
We confess that we have performed horrors and called them salvation. We have deluded ourselves into thinking that we are the heroes, that we are the saviors. Help us to become honest that we are the ones the world needs to be saved from. Empire has terrorized and erased so many expressions of the divine image in the name of "civilization." Mourn with us for the loss of cultural autonomy and the beauty that has been undone by colonialism. Reorient our global citizenship toward a reverence of the Indigenous, and an honoring of people and place, that we would at last contend with how the appetite of the powerful has led to an ecological crisis that lands heaviest on the backs of those nations historically excluded from power. Reveal and indict the greed that propels foreign policy. May the intruder in all his forms be caught and cast out before he claims more of what was never his to claim. Raise legions of peacemakers and truth-tellers to dismantle the unholy union of white supremacy and imperialism. Expand our capacity for empathy beyond our borders and across languages, that a virtue of respect would grow in us. We are not the heroes. Protect them from us. *Amen.*

FOR HEALING FROM CHURCH ABUSE

Divine Shelter,
Who can we trust? The origins of so many wounds are leaders who habitually abuse their spiritual authority. Spaces that demand our fealty and faith have been breeding grounds for abuse of all kinds. Reveal their false moral superiority. Spew from the pulpit the deceptive and power-thirsty. Expose them for who and what they are. Break every false teaching and attune the spiritually vulnerable to

the sound of their own voice. Lead us into new spaces of physical and spiritual safety where we can heal and connect and meet our pain and alienation with true belonging. Raise up new leaders— women, trans, queer, Black, disabled—people who understand collective power and collective liberation. *May it be so.*

FOR HEALTHY PARENTING

Sacred Guardian,
We confess that so much of our "parenting" is really a form of "controlling." There are times when we believe that we are more human than they—that our emotions are more valid, our needs more dire, our opinions more trustworthy. May we contend with this imbalance of power and the ways we perpetuate indignity in our homes by dismissing our children as inferior. The responsibility of parenting has humbled us, revealing complex relationships to authority, control, and fear from our own upbringings. Help us take our children seriously, never underestimating how our words can land on them, live in them. Grant us awareness of the things in our children that trigger us. Give us the courage to heal wounds left open from our own childhoods, as we seek to nurture the coming generation. Raise up communities to support single parents and those in poverty, that they would have all they need to parent free of shame. As we attune to our child selves who were dismissed, remind us that we do not have to resurrect methods of discipline that only made us feel smaller and more vulnerable than we already were. We do not have to love how we were loved. Teach us how to listen well and respect our children as fully human and worthy of power. *Amen.*

FOR DISMANTLING THE PATRIARCHY

God Our Mother,
We thank you for showing us what it is to be loved by the divine feminine. Millennia of patriarchal power have left the world aching and off balance. We have endured misogynoir and chauvin-

ism. We have endured a total demonization of female leadership under the delusion that we are too emotional. We feel the threat of men daily in our very bodies. Eradicate this disease that has crept out of our borders and into other lands. Scrape the scales from the eyes of those who find no fault with the history of male domination. Strengthen institutional revolutions around the world that overturn the power systems we've inherited. Catalyze the work in our own inner lives, that we would confront the biases in us as we perceive the world. Train us in the skills of deconstruction and decolonization, that we would challenge that subjugation which has been renamed "tradition." Remind us that we women possess an undeniable wisdom, savvy, and memory to lead this world on the journey to liberation. Gather our collective imaginations to fashion and nurture new ways of being human together. *May it be so.*

FOR THOSE WHO FEEL HELPLESS

God who reclaims,
We have known what it is to feel helpless. To have our agency stripped and voices snuffed out. We are grateful to those who have shown us that on the other side of our trauma, abuse, and grief, there can be power magnified. Bind the will of oppressors and abusers. Remember your promises to the vulnerable, poor, marginalized, and immigrant, to raise us up in honor and lead us from captivity. We have been forgotten for so long; do not forget us, God. Subvert the propaganda imparted by the white capitalist patriarchy and deliver us into a rich ecosystem of diverse power expressions. Speak gently into the hearts of those recently removed from harm. Keep us from punishing ourselves for what has been withheld from us. It is not our fault. We reclaim what's ours. *Amen.*

Breathe

INHALE: There is power in this breath.
EXHALE: There is agency in this body.

INHALE: Where can I go?
EXHALE: God, take me where it's safe.

INHALE: God, tear down the tyrant.
EXHALE: Lift up the healers.

Confession

Powerful God,
We confess that we have wielded power against one another, as opposed to using our power in protection of others. In a world of so much chaos and unpredictability, we have become feverish for any semblance of control, even if that control is used to neglect, exclude, and oppress others. We have pulled triggers, we have sent drones, we have sat by while powerful men wreak havoc on the world's most vulnerable. And our own daily power, we have used to maintain the status quo. We have stolen the bodily agency of others. We have dismissed the voices of our children and the elderly. For all that we've done or witnessed done, we are truly sorry. Forgive us and have mercy on us that we might know an empowered life, grounded in our own voices without suffocating those of others. *Amen.*

Forgiveness

Let your soul receive this rest: The God who wove order and direction into the very earth around us so too reveals all that they have relinquished control over. Allow the divine to restore your humanity to you, that you would turn from evil deeds and give that power which you have used so terribly to those who can be trusted to wield it well.

Benediction

May you wake and rest with humility in your hearts. May you be protected from the greed and fear that tempt us to dominate others. Possess such moral clarity that you would be able to be both leader and follower without threat to your sense of self. May you live responsibly and tenderly, that your power would never come at the expense of someone else's. *Amen.*

Contemplation

1. Are you more prone to trust or distrust of authority figures? When did this start for you?
2. Do you tend to assume the role of leader or follower? Does either role carry a negative connotation for you? Is this fair?
3. What is one area of your life where you feel that you are lacking agency? Who holds the power? What do you wish you could say to them without fear of retaliation?
4. Who is someone who makes you feel empowered? What have they done to leave you feeling that way?

JUSTICE

say it with your whole black mouth: i am innocent
& if you are not innocent, say this: i am worthy
of forgiveness, of breath after breath

—DANEZ SMITH

But if by some miracle, and all our struggle, the Earth is
spared, only justice to every living thing (and everything
alive) will save humankind. . . . Only justice can stop a
curse.

—ALICE WALKER

LETTER XV | TO ANYONE WHO ATE THAT SHIT

Justice is becoming one of those words that hurts on the way out of
me. To petition and hope for justice in a society predicated on corruption can feel futile and naïve. Lately it's felt almost embarrassing—
or is that shame?

On April 20, 2021, when police officer Derek Chauvin was found
guilty of murdering George Floyd, I felt nothing. I had prepared
myself for an acquittal but hadn't considered what coping would
still be necessary in the event he was found guilty. For months we
mourned and wrote letters, built altars, and restored memorials.
Many of us waited for the trial to offer some kind of resolve to the
utter restlessness that seeing another Black man murdered under
the weight of a white officer's knee catalyzed in us.

When the verdict was announced, I felt no relief. It didn't feel
triumphant; I felt no release in my chest which had grown tight
against my heartbeat. I felt no resolve. Floyd would not be restored
to his five children, to his friends and city. Just as Breonna Taylor
would not. And Sandra Bland, and Alton Sterling, and Philando

Castile, and Elijah McClain, and all others who deserve to be counted and named. They were still taken from us. There was no resurrection.

Sometimes I wonder if we lack imagination for any form of justice apart from punishment of the perpetrator. I think justice can contain this, but if this is all justice is, is it worth marching at all? Maybe so. But I want a justice that is just as concerned with rectifying the systems that allowed the injustice to take place. I want a death to whatever allowed Chauvin to kneel with a smirk at a half dozen phones recording as a man—a beautiful, dignified man— cried out for his mother. I want officers held accountable, yes, *and* I want policies changed. I want a total reckoning with the system of policing in a country where Black people have never been protected.

Justice, I think, will never feel enough. But I'm learning not to demean what justice we have access to in the present. I cannot afford to be dismissive of justice. My brothers, who both spent years in prison, cannot afford my hopelessness. My despair will not save them or me.

Zora Neale Hurston said, "If you are silent about your pain, they'll kill you and say you enjoyed it." If I can't have this pain resolved in full, I want to live so that the world cannot tell a different story about the blood that trails me. About the cages that hold the people I love. My protest, however that protest might look, will not resurrect the aunt who was taken from me because the medical system does not care about Black women bodies. But it will remind me of the power of my own Black woman body. It's more than just catharsis, it's a reclaiming.

More than two years after Breonna Taylor was unjustly shot six times and killed by Louisville, Kentucky, cops in the dead of night, federal charges were finally brought against four of the police officers involved. It took too long. We know this. And it was not a resurrection. In a statement, her mother, Tamika Palmer, said, "I've waited 874 days." She said, "It still hurts." She said, "Everything sent to break me, I ate that shit." Thirty-two bullets and a battering ram. A falsified warrant. 874 days. I cannot say what hope looks like for her, but I can say that no movement is sustained for more than two years by despair. Mrs. Palmer's statement contains no toxic positivity. "Everything sent to break me, I ate that shit." Which is to say, we will not be consumed.

I don't know what the world has been to you. I don't know those wicked things you've witnessed in the light and in the dark—the hand that grasps your throat even now. . . .

But I can tell you, you are not foolish for hoping. Don't let anyone make you feel ashamed for what fight remains in you. And may what has been emptied in you be found in me. I trust that when the time comes, you will hold my hope when I cannot.

Justice alone is not the destination. Becoming human is. This is liberation. We want no need for gavels, no need for sit-ins or philanthropy. No need for food drives or keys clenched between knuckles at night. We want more for ourselves.

But until then, we speak. We organize. We create. We hold hope for one another on the edge of despair, our voices sustained in the collective. Whether they listen or fail to listen, our mouth is ours. There is meaning in that.

Demanding more for you,
C

salvation

if you kill a man
it's your own blood he bleeds.

if you've saved a man
he's still saving you.

if you get everything you deserve
how afraid are you?

Prayers

FOR A JUSTICE SYSTEM THAT CANNOT BE TRUSTED

God Awake,

We are grateful that your love cannot be separated from truth-telling and justice. For too long we have known complacency and subjugation masquerading as love. Move us toward communities who are capable of the real thing. Our government, our justice system, our institutions, have been infiltrated and poisoned by empires whose only goal is the steady, desperate grasping for more power. Root this out. Raise up leaders who can kneel—who can draw near to those whose power has been overcome by socioeconomic injustice. Expose how evil our systems truly are. May all those we've pushed to the margins rise up and receive what has been stolen from them. May every prisoner remain grounded in their own dignity in a world that sells, trades, and forces them into unpaid labor. May every cop whose hand rushes to the trigger encounter the darkest parts of their own hearts before they discover it at our expense. May the wealthy contend with the utter void in their own interior worlds that causes them to devour resources and people in hopes of satiating an unfathomable greed. And God, reveal yourself as near to the brokenhearted, the suffering, the imprisoned, the impoverished and unloved. Make us agents of true restoration in a tired world. That we would commit ourselves to dismembering the schemes of injustice, in which love is never complicit. *Amen.*

FOR BEFORE A PROTEST

Defiant God,

If you were the voice of the prophets, then you remain a God who speaks against exploitation and oppression. Silence the lies in our minds that tell us our fight is futile. Let hope in our cause swell as we come together with a shared voice. Awaken our full emotional range, that our work would be fueled by a mysterious entanglement of righteous anger and defiant hope. May we heed the voice of our own interior prophets. Protect our bodies as we resist empire, especially the youngest and most vulnerable among us. Make our protests thoughtful and inclusive, as we submit to and learn from the disabled to create a diversity of paths to fight for justice. We ask that you soften the hearts of the unjust, not that we would view ourselves as responsible for their absolution, but with the awareness that there are times when the vilest of people can be shaken out of their heartlessness and into their humanity. Let us receive the inheritance of courage and steadfast dissent of our ancestors—that our steps would be their steps, our bodies their bodies, our protest a sacred echo as we boldly demand justice today. Sustain us, God. With every block we march, reveal us as forces for liberation in this world. *Ase.*

FOR VOTING

God of every voice,
Motivate us to use our own. We confess we are taken with the fashionable fatalism of our culture, which leaves us unprepared for the enduring nature of justice work. Help us to have compassion for all the memories that have formed us to feel this present helplessness. Renew our practice of love in community, that civic engagement would feel vital to us. Instill a commitment to local government, elevating the discussion of the common good in our immediate places of belonging. Surround our public leaders with wise counsel and a diversity of voices, that we would not elect leaders of arrogance and unchecked narcissism, however alluring their promises may be. Expose the status desperate, the power hungry, as politicians attempt to influence us to support them. Thwart all attempts at voter suppression, the evil schemes that uniquely target Black people, the overworked, and the elderly. Spur on young people of

color to pursue public service. Grant them the courage and resources to challenge officials who have failed at serving with their full humanity. Hold us in our purpose, that we would never become too accustomed to injustice. That we would never become numb to the pain of the world. This vote is only the beginning, but it is a sacred beginning. *May it be so.*

FOR LABOR UNIONS

United God,

We are scared to unite, yet we know this is the path to protection. Grant us courage to organize and come together, even under threat from our employers. Remind us that you are a God who views work as an expression of our dignity and identity in the world. The powerful and greedy have twisted work for their own gain, turning every man and woman against their labor and sowing injustice into our wages, working conditions, and benefits. Ground us in the long history of collective defiance in the working class. Renew our commitment to community, inspiring us to push back against the toxic individualism that changes nothing. Keep us from believing the propaganda that teaches us that power belongs to those with money and formal authority; remind us that the most important change comes from a collective voice. Converge the efforts of unions and those who work for racial and gender equality, as white patriarchal supremacy pervades all spheres of culture. And as we risk ourselves in union, grant rest to those who lead the work. Let our rights be protected. Let our bodies be honored. *May it be so.*

FOR THOSE TAUGHT TO BELIEVE IN SCARCITY

Abundant God,

Remind us that there is enough for us. We are grateful that the earth we have been entrusted to care for is one of beauty and provision. We have all we need. Reveal the hypocrisy and corruption of the privileged. In a world of men who have more than it would ever be humanly possible to spend, we have let entire countries starve and thirst, often because we have stolen the resources of their own sacred lands. Protect us from the myth of scarcity sold to us by white capitalism, which tells us we must fight for scraps because there is not enough. Rid us of the lie that the only way to contentment and survival is to sacrifice our bodies in work and toil. Expose the deception at work in our financial systems and economic processes. And help us tell new stories of what business and compensation might look like in a just society. Give us an imagination for a culture that leverages its resources for the protection of the vulnerable—human, creature, and land. Convict the overprivileged and wealthy to rend their own dignity and self-actualization from their possessions. And let those living in scarcity be reminded that there is enough for them. May they feel no guilt in claiming it. *Amen.*

FOR SOLIDARITY

God of Solidarity,

Thank you for being a God who enters the suffering of the world—who doesn't run from those in pain but rushes to the site of blood and tears. Release us from those empty cravings for unity that come at no cost to the oppressor. Lead us toward spaces of costly advocacy. We confess that in speaking up on behalf of the oppressed, we too soon become enamored with the sound of our own voices. Our egos spoil even our best intentions. Show us when the voices of the vulnerable are being drowned out by the cacophony of the privileged. Make our presence and dignity known in a world that perpetually eclipses the voices of the marginalized. Guide us into a solidarity that demands something of us. Let us learn to risk ourselves on behalf of the vulnerable, believing that when one of us is harmed, we all are. And God, keep us from those who will demonize the fight in us, who would prefer us complacent and far from one another. Secure in us the courage to resist, knowing that together we will restore what the world has tried to suffocate in us. *Amen.*

Breathe

INHALE: God, how long?
EXHALE: Justice is coming.

INHALE: We will not feel guilty for hope.
EXHALE: We'll accept nothing less than freedom.

INHALE: I will not make excuses for evil.
EXHALE: Consequence is holy.

Confession

Grieved God,
We are ashamed. We confess that we have not loved the way this world deserves. We have allowed children to starve. We have cast away generations of Black people behind bars, often for "crimes" that were necessary for our survival. We have been spineless about holding law enforcement accountable for their actions. We've been more concerned with performative activism and online diatribes than looking our own neighbor in the eye, than demanding more for the marginalized in our communities. We have not voted with compassion. We have not voted at all. We have changed our very benches to keep the homeless from their rest. We have exploited land and sea, allowing our own filth to colonize the deepest beauties of the world. As we contend with all the ways we've perverted the glory of the world, we hardly feel worthy of forgiveness. But we humbly ask that you would forgive us. Have mercy on us, all our heartlessness, that we would be filled again with the fullness of our humanity. *Amen.*

Forgiveness

Let your soul receive this rest: The God who sends thunder and lightning seeks to obliterate every system that threatens the dignity and shalom of the cosmos. Accept what mercy is available after what we've made of this precious sacred world—what we've made of one another. In all our greed, our deceit, our apathy, our moral deficiencies, may the divine forgive us, and work so that that every injustice would at last be made right. *Amen.*

Benediction

Go with heads bowed, in humility toward all you have done and not done to protect every living thing. May you be sewn into the complicated tapestry of oppressed and oppressor, knowing you are more than one thing. May you march and write and sing and educate and use what power you have to call forth justice. And may you contend daily with all the ways the curse still dwells in the hidden parts of you, that you would be a person of constant searching, self-honesty, confession, and forgiveness. *Amen.*

Contemplation

1. In what ways has the myth of scarcity been taught to you? How does it feel to claim "enough" for yourself? Explore any guilt or renewal when you do so.
2. Explore the connection between justice and liberation. Has one been centered over the other in your communities? How has this formed you?
3. What loves or gifts could you use toward justice and liberation?
4. When have you encountered despair in either yourself or another? What facilitated the movement out of hopelessness?
5. What cause is near to you in this season? Write out your hopes without placing constraints on them.
6. Where can you speak compassion over yourself for exhaustion in justice work? What would a sustainable balance look like?

16

REPAIR

Are you sure, sweetheart, that you want to be well? . . . Just
so's you're sure, sweetheart, and ready to be healed, cause
wholeness is no trifling matter. A lot of weight when
you're well. —TONI CADE BAMBARA

I shall become a collector of me. . . .
I shall Become A COLLECTOR of me.
I SHALL BECOME A COLLECTOR OF ME. . . .
AND PUT MEAT ON MY SOUL.

—SONIA SANCHEZ

LETTER XVI | TO THOSE MARKED BY ASH

I'm writing to you to try to convince myself it's okay to not forgive
them.

I had a friend whose mother would make her and her sister slip
a single XL T-shirt over both their tiny bodies whenever they got
into a fight as kids. They would sit shoulder to shoulder, squirming
in each other's nearness, until one of them apologized and they
were ready to hug and make up. I remain fascinated by this. Apparently, the parental strategy is not uncommon. When I asked her if
it worked, she replied, *For who?*

She disclosed that often she and her sister would continue to
poke and pinch each other underneath the shared shirt. But when
their mom's eye drifted toward them, they'd pretend nothing was
wrong and they weren't hurting beneath. Eventually, they did always find a way back to each other, but it was on their own terms.
Once they knew they could trust the remorse in the other's voice or
face. This is the beginning of a question. Why do we presume that

proximity will result in reconciliation? And if reconciliation is forced, can it be true?

I used to work for an organization that hated me, both my Blackness and my queerness. Those with any real power were so content with toxic white evangelicalism that any challenge to them was seen as a challenge to God. I stayed longer than I care to admit. There was a growing group of people of color who had tricked ourselves (or perhaps been tricked) into thinking we could exact meaningful change. We served on panels and led trainings. We met with board members and VPs. Our brains were picked. Our words were used. And at the end of the day, we were still hated. Until there was an uprising.

An anonymous website was created, documenting racist and homophobic abuse employees had endured, and calling for the termination of particular people in leadership. We called them by name, those who sat in meetings telling us our anger was sinful, those who made crude jokes and justified them, those who financially oppressed us, those who touched our bodies, who threatened our job mobility when we told the truth. Those who, upon learning that a white theologian had hit a Black woman in the middle of a training, chose to wear that same man's face on T-shirts at a banquet a month later to "honor" him. We called them by name, and then opened a submission form for others to share stories. It was a scandal, with donors and board members and other staff devolving into crisis. Some thought it brilliant, necessary. *At last.* Others thought it cruel. *Isn't there a better way to go about all of this? So many people will be affected.*

In the days that followed, a hunt began. The question of course was not who was responsible for the toxic acts detailed in the stories; rather, who was responsible for telling the stories? Who made the site? No one said a word. The irony being that no one *needed* to say a word because everyone knew. Those named and unnamed had long known the pain of the storytellers; they had met with them, they had dismissed them, they had labeled them "not good fits." So on the morning the site went live, there was never a question of who did it, only a question of how will they be caught.

As the days went on, my personal email began to fill up with questions, usually containing the word "reconciliation." People wanted us to find resolution. To all come together again. *For the body of Christ.* Some said, *This is not the way to go about it. We are family,* they said. The president, teary-eyed and brow furrowed, pleaded with the staff to be patient. Asked staff of color to come forward and talk. To *reconcile.*

But our sharing of those stories was not a step toward reconciling. It was an act of sacred destruction. A dismantling. Shortly after, Black staff and other staff of color remaining in the organization began to depart in waves. Some remained. My heart goes out to them.

Too often we are asked to participate in a form of repair that is synonymous with uniting. We are asked to become one again with our wounder or oppressor with no evidence that they've done anything to change.

I told my story with no desire to repair relationships. I told my story to repair myself. To reclaim the person who had convinced herself it was okay to accept crumbs at a table that was never set for her. Sometimes the reconciliation we are after is, in fact, with the self.

What is needed for healing? Apology? I received none. Forgiveness? I gave none. Healing is far more complicated and mysterious than this. It's both memory and liberation. It's acknowledging the bleeding and then resting and tending to the wound long enough for it to scab over. It's tracing the scars, those done to us and those we've done ourselves. It's being held again but by hands you can trust.

I cannot say how it will happen to you, but I can tell you time is its own miracle. It's okay if you had to burn it down. Some ashes make the soil come alive again.

Stay near to yourself,

C

healing an abandonment wound

If they wanted to, the crows outside your window could leave you with the nest and its screeching contents. How do birds know which branches can hold them? The African jacana lays her eggs on nests that float on water like lily pads. Her island of stems and leaves, a perpetual site of repair. How much it can hold without sinking is the wisdom of the female's body. She who knows precisely where to place the weight to keep from sending it tipping altogether into the lagoon. Who taught her how to make a raft in the deep? Every step a negotiation with the mirrored surface. Slender legs walking on water, all things mending.

Prayers

FOR THERAPY

God who listens,
Too often we have been falsely promised healing from God and God alone. We have been alienated from those who can help us, and plagued by shame for needing more than what prayer was meant to provide. Release us from the narrative that our only path to healing is in the supernatural or invisible form of God. Show us the divine in our own agency. Be with us who have entrusted our stories and interior worlds to therapists. May our therapists be safe—intuitive, compassionate, and forthright. Raise up new voices in the fields of psychology and psychiatry to continue to untether these disciplines from white norms and expectations. Help us to take seriously other healers and historic practices of communal care. Recenter the body in the work of mental and emotional healing. So many of us have attempted to wander alone in our journey back to ourselves. Release us from the idea that self-sufficiency is a virtue, especially in our emotional and mental health. Grant us the courage required to seek help. Not only help in crisis, but support as we process the lives we've lived and the liberation we want. *May it be so.*

FOR REPARATIONS

God who mends,
You demand of us not merely justice, but repair. We confess that we have reduced reconciliation to niceties and "unity" out of fear for what it might actually cost a person. Expose this, so that we can be people of true repair—people who demand an accounting for the rubble left by our histories, who possess a sacred imagination for how we might bring reparations in our country, cities, and neighborhoods. Give white people the courage to become honest about

what they've stolen and what must be returned. And grant us the liberation necessary to ask for what we need, to ask for justice not merely in the vaguely moral, but with grave specificity in the economic chasms that whiteness has created. We want more. And we claim it. *Ase.*

FOR WHEN YOU GROW TOO FAMILIAR WITH HURTING

Healer God,
Some of us don't know who we are when we are not in pain. We've spent so much time proving our ache that it has become all we can remember. Help us to honor the truth of our struggle and still pursue healing. Remind us that repair is not erasure. That as we heal, there is no less compassion or grief available to us. That when we forgive, we do not say the harm was okay, only that we no longer wish to be contained by it. We've known suffering for so long that to hope for anything else can be a portal to more disappointment. Protect us from becoming so disillusioned with hope that we are unable to recognize healing when it meets us. Remind us that we are so much more than our pain. We will not be reduced. Reacquaint us with the sight of our whole face. *Amen.*

FOR EMBODIED HEALING

God of every ache,
Help us to befriend our bodies. We confess that it is easy to turn against them as the source of our struggle. Awaken a compassion, a tenderness, toward the parts of us that are changing, hurting—remembering that our bodies are doing everything they can to protect us, to hold back the pain and exhaustion. With every ailing and unseen thing, guide us toward those capable of listening and perceiving when we are not okay, that we wouldn't feel pressure to pretend or apologize or explain. Remind us that we are not a burden but a beacon to those who are so poorly attuned to their own bodies and needs that they have forgotten what self-compassion

looks like. Help us exist in the truth of what we need. Hold us in love as we resist the demands of this world. *Amen.*

FOR INTERGENERATIONAL HEALING

Sacred Origin,

By story and by blood, we are made of those who came before us. Too often our false ideas of healing cause us to reject the past, distancing us from our own stories. Show us how liberation stretches out in both directions, past and future. Assure us that what has been does not always have to be. Train us in new coping habits, new patterns of self-regulation that counter what we think we are destined for. Center storytelling and exchange in our family system, that we would learn to be gentle with those memories that feel tender and fragile and be strengthened by the miracle of our survival. Keep us from living into dysfunctional family roles, that no one would be held captive by what an unhealthy family decides is their identity. Sow compassion and curiosity and a sacred transience in us, that we would meet one another again and again in new seasons of life. Affirm the need for collective remembrance and processing, protecting those stories that are prone to being forgotten or misremembered. But remind us that our processing need not be rushed—that we can go slowly, taking time to tend to our wounds. To travel into the trauma of past generations is costly; may we do so carefully, and with a companion who is safe and trustworthy. *Ase.*

Breathe

INHALE: Healing is after me.
EXHALE: I am ready to be well.

INHALE: I am more than pain.
EXHALE: Tragedy is not my name.

INHALE: God, restore me to myself.
EXHALE: Let this breath be a mending.

Confession

God of renewal,
We confess that too often we have desired justice without repair.
Liberation without healing. We have purged our stories of nuance,
and exalted tragedy as the most important thing. Other times we
have demanded a rushed unity of the oppressed, without fully
contending with all the ways the union is still to their demise. We
have not offered meaningful reparations, choosing to retain wealth
that never really belonged to us. And, as for our own healing, we
are terrified. We confess that we forget who we are when we aren't
hurting. We want more for ourselves, but something keeps pulling
us back to loveless places. Have mercy on us in our resistance, that
we would pursue repair and enter the healing we were meant for.
Amen.

Forgiveness

Let your soul receive this rest: The God who resurrects the trees
and the grass has mercy on the death of this world, including our
own interior decay. They seek to mend the brokenhearted, provide
for the economically oppressed, honor the aging, and protect the
vulnerable. Receive forgiveness for the injustices you've participated in and be purged of those that still reside in your own heart.
Find renewal in the divine, that we would welcome healing as it
knocks. That we would reintegrate every part of us that this world
has tried to cleave apart, claiming the dignity of our bodies daily. As
you receive this mercy, let it hold you and keep you, that your hope
for liberation would be reborn each morning. *Amen.*

Benediction

May you practice a sacred reclamation of all this world was made
for—dignity, love, belonging, delight. May you nurture your own
imagination for repair in all its forms, and expand with self-

compassion, in the knowledge that no healing is linear, and no reparation final. *Amen.*

Contemplation

1. What has been your experience with reconciliation? Are you prone to rushing to resolution? Why or why not?
2. How have you seen concepts of unity weaponized against the vulnerable?
3. Where have you seen repair practiced well? What made it sincere?
4. What does healing in relationship to the body look like for you? How can you heal your relationship with your body without demanding anything from it?

1 7

REST

There is no end
To what a living world
Will demand of you.

—OCTAVIA BUTLER

I don't want a seat at the table of the oppressor. I want a
blanket and pillow down by the ocean. I want to rest.

—TRICIA HERSEY

LETTER XVII | TO THOSE IN NEED OF A LULLABY

If you are receiving these letters in order, you know by now that the night does not guarantee me rest. It is 3:48 A.M. right now. My body woke me almost two hours ago, and, losing hope of being able to fall back asleep, I at last grabbed my journal and began to write you.

Admittedly, I feel some degree of guilt for this, as someone who spends her days asking people to listen to their bodies, to liberate themselves from the bondage of capitalism and exhaustion. No one warns you that listening to your body can be costly if you're chronically ill. My forearms are twitching like popcorn under heat, and I've already had to take a few breaks for the burning in my hands to subside. My body is tired. But it's also wired. There's an alertness in me marked by the fact that I keep seeing things in my periphery and I'm sweating like I've just sprinted down the block and I've imagined having a conversation I'll never actually have a dozen or so times on repeat. I'm so tired I could cry. But what do we do when our bodies or minds can't access rest, even when we posture it?

For one, I've chosen silence. I could turn on some sad, slow music and hope that it would put me to sleep. For some, this works. But I've learned the language of my body enough to know that, for me, music is only a soundtrack for an anxious mind. I'll have that conversation a dozen times more, only it will be put to music, made as real as a movie. It may be different for you. Perhaps music is your lullaby, but the point is that you would pay attention enough to realize it as such. For me, in this silence, I am steadied. The noise of my mind grows loud at first, but in the silence its loudness becomes so stark, I cannot help but contend with it. Silence leaves no place for denial. And so, it is in silence—listening to some creature crunch through the snow outside my window, listening to my own staggered breath—that I realize one of the causes for my restlessness. I see it more clearly. And I remember I am free to walk away from this conversation I will never actually have. I've learned I cannot empty my mind (for an emptied mind will always find something to fill it), but I can reclaim it with a different, more restful conversation.

Second, I've chosen darkness. Lately, I've been trying not to rip myself fully into the land of the conscious with the light of my computer screen. Some nights I do. But tonight I chose my journal so that I could avoid turning on the light. I hardly know if this letter will be legible come morning because I can hardly make out where the next line should begin. This is okay. It is in the darkness that I am reminded of darkness's beauty. In a body that is hyperalert, this moment alone in the dark is a kind of rest. It narrows my vision, keeps me from being able to see more than I should be alert to. I must be content with the hidden. I cannot make out the doorknob or the muscles twitching beneath my skin, I can only see the words before me, the pen in my own hand. In a way, I am calmed by this.

There is a reason you can't bring yourself to close the laptop, to walk away from your work, to close your eyes. How terrifying might rest appear to a woman who is working three jobs to pay her rent? To those who fear homelessness or hunger or punishment if they do not produce for these toxic systems? We belong to a society that claims ownership over our bodies, that across generations has used our bodies for its own ends. Our petitions for rest cannot be grounded in self-help wellness talks that don't recognize this reality.

Tricia Hersey wrote, "[I refuse] to donate my body to a system that still owes a debt to my Ancestors." This is how we account for the restlessness of the world. By naming the oppressive, greed-stricken capitalistic culture that sowed it in us. By naming the stories of trauma and abuse our bodies have endured. By remembering that this anxiety ricocheting through your body at three A.M. has an origin. And the origin is not you.

I want sleep for you. Deep, dream-bearing sleep. But if the restlessness of the world has done damage that cannot immediately be undone, have compassion for yourself. It's not your fault the dreams won't come. Your body is doing the best it can in a world that has used it far more than it has loved it.

No healing is immediate, and it's rarely ever linear. Some days you'll dream your ancestors back to life, and other days it's you and the cold sweats and the darkness and racing thoughts. It's not your fault. Somebody should've told you it's not your fault.

It's past four now and the birds are waking. It's time for us. Lie down with me and don't apologize. Quiet now. This dark, for however long it lasts, can also be our harbor. I'm breathing with you. Let our bodies be our lullaby.

Dreaming with you,
C

the cocoon is not a cage

Your palm
On your chest while your heart slows

Your breath
Warming the air under your grandmother's quilt

You rest for everyone who couldn't
Satin crown defiant

I wish I knew how silence
Sounds to you

Prayers

FOR BOUNDARIES

God of boundaries,
Remind us that sometimes we need to walk away from people and situations for our own rest and survival. That when the demands of the world grow loud, we have full agency to choose silence and peace. The stories we tell ourselves about why we cannot do so are often grounded in guilt—a guilt that has been carefully implanted by a society that believes we are products to be used and consumed. We have been pushed and pulled out of ourselves and our own desires. Grant us the courage to say "no" without apology, that we would meet the demands of this world with truth-telling and self-charity, knowing that our boundaries are holy ground. We will not survive by inching further and further away from safety. Show us that sometimes the boundary we fear setting marks the border between freedom and bondage. Be with us on the journey back to a solid voice. When we speak *no*, let it shatter chains. *Ase.*

FOR WHEN REST FEELS LIKE A RISK

Rested God,
We want more than a life lived exhausted. That you have woven healing rhythms of rest into our minds and bodies reminds us we are worthy of habitual restoration. Keep us from apologizing for our own healing, that we would know that when we pause or rest, we are restoring not only our own bodies but the very condition of a world held captive by greed and utility. We grow weary of societies who view us as more machine than human, more product than soul. The fear that we won't survive without overworking stalks our days. Liberate us from the depraved socioeconomic structures that require that the poor and vulnerable sacrifice their own rest at the

altar of survival and opportunity. Protect us from fear as we rest with you, breathe with you. Remind us that the beauty and paradox of our humanness is that we were made to close our eyes, that we might see. *May it be so.*

FOR INSOMNIA

God of the long night,
Every part of us is weary. The fatigue from sleepless nights is too much for us to hold. We are desperate to rest, yet it feels impossible to access. We have endured critique, unsolicited advice, and judgment from those who insinuate that we are to blame for our exhaustion. Keep us from any guilt that we are unable to care for ourselves the way that we want to. Meet us in our bodies tonight, that we would become protectors of their needs in a world that does not always understand them. Meet us in the stillness, that we would become so acquainted with quiet that in it, we could perceive your tenderness and love. Help us to reimagine what rest could look like for us, opening us to other forms of relaxation and meditation. Stay up with us, God. That even when rest seems so cruelly off course, we would be assured that the divine is near to us. Wait up with us until rest finds its way home. *Amen.*

FOR THOSE WHO'VE FORGOTTEN HOW TO PLAY

God of levity,
Grant us a rest that permeates our waking hours. Mark our days with the recreation and playfulness of our youth. Restore to us the energy for mischief and creativity and competition that we've lost as we've gotten older. Put people in our lives who inspire us in our play. Game nights, karaoke, gardening, film—we want more than the binary of work and sleep. We want delight in the in-between, those moments of interior rest that can happen while we're awake. Show us what forms of entertainment and what hobbies lead us

into peace. And protect us from the lie that if we are awake, we should be working. Remind us that a light heart is not a heart that lacks depth. That our play does not negate our grief. Let us rest in the way we need to today. *Amen.*

FOR BLACK WOMEN WHO WERE TAUGHT THEY WERE RESPONSIBLE FOR SAVING THE WORLD

Sacred Peace,

We're not saving this. Too often we are expected to rescue the world from its own ugliness—to save our communities, our elections, our churches, our relationships, our men. We are used as teacher, prophet, priest, and therapist, all without compensation. We are tired. Let us reclaim ourselves. Help us to resist a society that uses Black women to alleviate its own guilt. Expose those in our lives who see us as more resource than human. Show the world the ways it uses us as mere tools for others' own self-realization. We don't want to be bridges, trampled on daily so that folk can be guided across deep waters without ever getting wet. We want to be human—whole, complicated, rested, and well. Draw us near to those who are disinterested in our utility and grant us courage to walk away from those our intuition continues to warn us against. We want more for ourselves. More rest, more laughter, more play, more adventure. Be our peace in a desperate world. *Ase.*

FOR COLLECTIVE CARE

Loving God,

We confess that we are so accustomed to pushing through an exhausted state that we come to expect the same from those nearest to us. We mirror the demands made of us and dissociate from the reality that these demands have harmed us, have left us anxious and unwell. Reorient our souls toward more than self-care. We want more for one another than the same expectations that haunt us, the same brutal experience of living within the systems of this world. Free us from resentment and envy as we bear witness to the prophets in our lives who practice rest and boundaries well. Let them be our guides into deeper freedom. Help us to never get used to being used. We were made for more. And together we possess the mysterious power of regeneration wrapped up in our bones. *May it be so.*

Breathe

INHALE: I deserve more than exhaustion.
EXHALE: I return home to myself.

INHALE: May I rest,
EXHALE: that I might dream.

INHALE: I've given enough.
EXHALE: I choose rest.

Confession

God of the night,
We confess that we have chosen exhaustion over dreaming. We have been tricked and indoctrinated into systems of dehumanization that allow the most vulnerable to work far more than their bodies ever should. We have set up an economy that demands we sacrifice ourselves at the altars of productivity and utility, that says we won't survive without our overwork. We have traded our own peace, our communion with our own interior landscapes, for the frenzied noise of an exhausted world. Even as we sense our own desperation for rest, we have still demanded exhaustion from those in our midst, welcoming them into the same chains that bind us. Forgive us. And have mercy on our weary souls, that we would locate the holy quiet, the divine lullaby that whispers within each of us, *You've given enough; you are worthy of rest. Amen.*

Forgiveness

Let your soul receive this rest: The God who sends the sun to sleep each night without apology, so too grants you the rest that has been withheld from you and your ancestors. She forgives us all our restlessness, that we would no longer be tormented by silence and stillness but find it a sacred reprieve from a world whose demand on our bodies is loud and unceasing. *Amen.*

Benediction

Go in courage to lie down, in sacred defiance of a world that would rather own your body than protect it. May you say "no" and "I'm leaving" and "I'm not saving this," your boundaries never predicated on apology. In a time of frenzied activity, may you choose stillness, and this breath, and this silence . . . and sleep, that you might dream. *Amen.*

Contemplation

1. What were your guardians' relationships to rest growing up? How has this formed you (in resistance to or in alignment with)?
2. If rest feels like a risk or threat to you, explore why that could be. What is at stake if you choose rest over exhaustion?
3. How do you contribute to the exhaustion of the world? Are there any expectations you have for your community that you yourself have experienced as a burden?
4. Who in your life do you resent for resting well? What do they possess that you wish you could access?
5. What is your relationship to rest in this season? In addition to adequate sleeping, dream up other rituals of rest for yourself.

J O Y

it is not unusual to sift
through ashes
and find an unburnt picture

—NIKKI GIOVANNI

Life is a hard battle anyway. If we laugh and sing a little
as we fight the good fight of freedom, it makes it all go
easier.   —SOJOURNER TRUTH

LETTER XVIII | TO THE ONES WHO DON'T FLOAT

A few years ago, a friend told me I tend to dislike happy people. I objected at first. But when I took account of my closest friends, it seemed that each of them in their own way possessed a sort of solemnity. None, I would say, are lighthearted in nature. And while we laugh together, it would be stranger for our conversations to lack gravity than humor.

So when I met Esther, who giggles like SpongeBob and walks like she's skating, I knew I mustn't retreat. We met through a mutual friend. The first time we had dinner, she laughed at her own jokes like she was watching stand-up. She didn't wait for me to laugh first, like some; she was present to herself in that way. And I sat there and watched as the goofiest things began to leak out of me in her presence. It didn't feel like she was giving me permission so much as she had unlocked a part of me. I didn't have to walk through a door; I didn't have to work for it. Levity came to me. A fraction of hers, but there nonetheless.

When we became roommates, I anticipated seeing her mask slip, that her happiness would be revealed as charade. I wouldn't have blamed her for this; I already loved her far too deeply by then. But

I found quite the opposite occurred. The more I got to know her, the more real her happiness became to me. She claps for herself after parallel parking, even when we land miles from the curb. She cooks feasts with rotten produce, believing things once good are always worth trying to revive.

The thing about Esther, the thing that is not immediately apparent to those who encounter her, is that she does possess a profound sorrow. She has experienced too much grief for one life. I wonder if she would even call herself happy. But Esther taught me what it means to be a person of deep pain without letting it eclipse every part of oneself. She contains the miracle of both joy *and* happiness. Joy being a quality of one's interior life. And happiness being the courage to let exterior circumstances still raise one's spirits. Perhaps I didn't like happy people because I thought joy could only have one face, and it would never be my own.

I didn't become Esther. I'm still not giggly and I don't get excited over the "little" things. Still, in the presence of her joy, I became more myself. At peace. Solid. A little lighter. Silly in strange ways. More aware that no day is only ever tragedy. Zadie Smith wrote, "You are never stronger . . . than when you land on the other side of despair." I think joy gets us there. And when we wander, it calls us back home before nightfall.

I'm writing to let you know that you are more than your pain. That you can feel deeply without being consumed. For you, I want laughter. And if you cannot locate your laughter, may you find some dispensation of comfort. I need you to survive this terrible, beautiful place. Sorrow alone will starve you.

Your joy doesn't need to look like mine, but what is tethering you to the beautiful? You've seen the fires burning, stared down the dragon's gaping mouth. Tell me, what is keeping you here? Steadying your breath in weary places? This resistance, this entrance to a world of our own remaking—if you're suspended in the tension, who says you can't make music?

Breathe easy,

C

missing the bus on purpose

sitting on your porch
one leg in sun and one in shade,
light splitting through you
like Picasso's face.

solving this
cryptogram I made and laughing how
that symbol reminds us
of your mom's bent menorah
that lets the candles slip out,
but she won't throw it away
because the patina reminds her
of the empty steel mill.

when it began to snow, and nothing made sense,
and I didn't know how
to ask you to stay
but you did,
handing me the pen with a shiver.

and we don't look at the time,
and we're anything but afraid.

We know peace
When the sky is falling.
Love, in your crossed eyes, refracting.

Prayers

FOR A JOY THAT TRANSCENDS

Honest God,
We don't want to fake it. We can't go on with forced smiles and feigned laughter when happiness seems so far from us. The weight of the world is so heavy, it feels as if we don't have any strength left to carry joy along with it. Be with us now as we try to reclaim and attune to some beauty in the world. Keep us from despair. Let joy be the arms that carry us from hopelessness. Not that we would have to manufacture our own happiness, but that a mysterious peace would comfort us, that joy itself would be the ground beneath our feet when we feel weary. Grant us emotional honesty on the journey, knowing you will never ask us to dismiss our pain; rather, you ensure that our pain doesn't consume us. Remind us that more than one thing can be true at once. That the world can be terrible and still dare to be beautiful. In the fight against oppression in all its forms, may joy protect us. *Amen.*

FOR THE TABLE

God of the table,
Meet us as we gather. As we recline at the table, help us to make space to delight in the sacred community we've been given. For the time we're here, let us look up and truly see one another's faces. Protect the comedy of us—the jokes, the playfulness, every smirk or raised eyebrow. As laughter rings out from us—chairs rocked back, tears in our eyes, gasping for breath—pause time. Pause time and allow the sacredness of the moment to be realized. Remind us that it's not laughter alone that is the cure, but laughter shared—joy in community, saving our people again and again. Keep us from becoming too serious. Let our children watch us delight in each

other, tease each other, embrace each other. And may this table be the site of memory, passed down from generation to generation, that our children would learn the sound of their own laughter in us. Right here. *Amen.*

FOR DANCING

God who moves,
Let joy make a home in this flesh. We confess that in our activism and pursuit of justice we can become so serious, so emptied of play, that we become one-dimensional and stagnant. Shake us from within. Help us to remember the greats, those who showed us what resistance looked like on the dance floor, those who made time to have fun. When we hear the music, send the beat to restore us, bass pulsing through us and in us, connecting us to one another. When we move and dip and sway, let us remember we have agency over these bodies, freedom in these hips. We don't have to obey. Help us listen to ourselves, our intuition, and let our bodies do what they need to do. Let all our movement be a holy signal that we are still here, alive and in rhythm. *Ase.*

FOR JOY THAT HAD TO BE HIDDEN

God of the laughing barrel,
Joy shouldn't have to be hidden. We make space for our ancestors who had to contain demonstrations of joy and happiness to survive; who once laughed into barrels to avoid the wrath of their enslavers. Help us to remember that we descend from those who were able to preserve humor amid terrible evil. Ancestors who let joy possess their bodies at great risk to them. As we struggle with our own sorrows, remind us that joy and pain are not exclusive. Let our laugh be defiant, in resistance to all who have dared to attempt to suppress it. May those who only wish to see our grief be disappointed and laid bare, that we would mystify the world with a sa-

cred sound. That we would laugh loud, without fear, for those who couldn't. *Ase.*

FOR BLACK TWITTER

God in public,
We are grateful for all the ways you demonstrate a playfulness in the world. Let us continue to claim a divine levity in private and in public, multiplying it before one another in unexpected times. Our joy is contagious, rippling out of us even when we are not in physical proximity to other people. Remind us always that we made community out of an app that was not meant for us. That we found laughter under the harshest duress. Help us to never forget the power of Blackness in community with itself, that whether it be on Twitter or around the table, at birthday parties or homegoings, we would know that we possess a mysterious access to joy. Let us never stop being us. Let us laugh with one mouth. *Amen.*

Breathe

INHALE: I am more than my pain.
EXHALE: I will not be reduced.

INHALE: I honor my story.
EXHALE: This joy carries memory.

INHALE: I claim joy.
EXHALE: I am filled.

Confession

Whole God,
We confess that we have paid so little attention to the sources of joy in our daily lives. We have such constant access to the terrors and traumas of this world that it has become difficult to see anything else. We have sneered and mocked the happiness of others, dismiss-

ing their fun as immature or juvenile. We have possessed sparse imagination for the relationship between sorrow and joy, often demanding joy present as mere cheerfulness. We have grown so used to the sinister curiosity around Black pain, that we've created a culture where it is consumed as the only Black experience worth attuning to. Liberate us, God. And have mercy on our imbalanced assessment of daily life, that in our survival we would cling to the practices of joy we've inherited and find some measure of peace. *Amen.*

Forgiveness

Let your soul receive this rest: The God of joy takes compassion on your inner doom and fills you with a peace that surpasses understanding. Let the divine guide you to laugh, joke, rest, dance, remember, dream, all steadied by a belief that you are worthy of goodness even when goodness does not immediately make herself known to you. Forgive yourself your despair and relax in the arms of the divine. *Amen.*

Benediction

Be at peace. May you access the fullness of a joy that allows for both an interior solemnity and a levity. May you learn to be at rest with yourself, able to access a peace that carries memory but isn't chained to the past. And may you laugh, allowing the mystery of joy to steady you always and keep you from despair. *Amen.*

Contemplation

1. How do you distinguish joy and happiness in you? What helps you access each?
2. What has your experience been with toxic positivity? When have you been tempted to perpetuate it?
3. Explore a time when you felt a deep inner peace. Are you prone

to searching for peace or letting it find you? Why do you think this is?

4. Where or how do you experience joy in your body? What do you notice?

5. What role does humor play in your relationships? How can you pursue levity as a virtue?

L O V E

Love takes off the masks that we fear we cannot live without and know we cannot live within.

—JAMES BALDWIN

you can't make homes out of human beings
someone should have already told you that
and if he wants to leave
then let him leave
you are terrifying
and strange and beautiful
something not everyone knows how to love.

—WARSAN SHIRE

LETTER XIX | TO THE SOULS IN OPEN WATER

Two people in the middle of the ocean drifting farther and farther from shore. One underwater, the other floating. The voice of the one above cuts through the surface of the water and says, *Grab hold of my hand, I'll lift you up.* The one sinking looks up and with their last breath says, *How could I? I'd pull you under.* The water is both their salvation and their death.

Do you know how people say they love something so much it hurts? I used to think this meant the relationship was toxic, that the person they loved was doing the hurting. It took time for me to understand that sometimes love hurts because you're terrified, and anticipating the loss of someone is nearly as painful as losing them. It stretches the grief out across time and transcends linearity. For this reason, many of us would rather lose love than wait to lose it. We swim away. Others turn to desperation. We cling to the other person for dear life, our interior lives frenzied, as we try to make our love someone else's salvation. I do not need to tell you how danger-ous this can be when one of the parties is abusive. We'll endure all kinds of things when we are bracing for total loss. The end of the world has a way of limiting our imaginations.

I knew someone who thought their love could save me. They thought with enough affirmation and romanticism, I'd get out of bed or stop cringing at the sight of my own face in the mirror. Mov-ies idealize this type of love. In real life, it didn't feel good to be loved by someone trying to save me. And I suspect it didn't feel good for them to love a person they were desperate to save but who re-mained drowning.

Maybe love was never meant to save us. Or kill us. Two people in an ocean, drifting in and out of reach. Maybe love is the sound of the waves against their bodies, traveling back and forth in the space between them. It is knowing that the same wave that meets my body meets yours, and we have chosen to be near enough to be held by the same terrible, beautiful waters.

Who will hold you when the ocean floor is dispersing from un-derneath you? When your skin is shriveled up like a raisin in sun? You are nobody's savior and nobody's burden; you are near. Near enough to hear your friend's last gasp. Near enough to watch the shimmering water raise them up on high.

From sea,

C

Moesha

I should've known when I began
Tangling legs with sierra palmer
Under covers marked
With chocolate and licorice.
When I wanted to touch
Her face, soft and clear.
When I wanted to be her face—

But it was years
Later, sitting
In front of the television,
A girl with box braids
And a raspy voice whips
Her head toward me
And my breath catches on the corner
Of the suede rocker and glides back into me
Particles down my widest
River alternating
And I remember myself.

This static light between us
Passing through my surface,
Love is a current
She is my conductor.

Prayers

FOR FALLING IN LOVE

God who rises,
This feels good. This feels terrifying. No one tells us that love feels so much like fear. Help us to love without being consumed. Awaken in us a sense of pleasure and play. When our palms sweat, when our bellies flicker, let us never demean the giddiness in us. And if we feel nothing at all, may this too be beautiful, knowing that we don't have to force what doesn't move us, and we don't have to feel our heart race in order to choose love. Would you grant us the wisdom of Toni Morrison, who wrote, "I didn't fall in love, I rose in it. I saw you and made up my mind." Help us toward the kind of love that is decisive. A love that may include giddy beginnings but is much more than an affectionate whim. Let us choose love. And in return, be chosen—again and always. *Amen.*

FOR LOVING CHILDREN

God our maker,
We want to love well. That we have been entrusted to care for children is a responsibility not lost on us. We have agonized over the gap between who we are and who they need us to be. Help us unlearn the ways we've been formed to control rather than nurture, to manipulate rather than guide. Remind us that endless self-sacrifice, however noble it may feel, can traumatize and leave us aching and exhausted. Teach us how to honor our own needs and desires, that in doing so we would demonstrate what it means to survive in a world of so much resentment and disembodiment. Gather community around us for accountability and insight. May any failure we feel be met with compassion, and the same patience we pray to have with our children, may we also have with ourselves. Protect these sacred bonds, God. Keep them near enough that we will always

hear them when they need us, but never so close that we smother or suffocate. Show us the mutuality available to us across age. That as we raise and teach them, we would learn and grow from them as well, as we bear witness to their wonder, curiosity, and wisdom. *Amen.*

FOR SIBLINGS

Bonded God,

We thank you for the gift of siblings. Help us to honor the unique ways we are formed by their presence. We thank you for the siblings who protected us, those who included us, those who raised us. Remind us of all that we've journeyed through together. Protect the memory of our laughter, our play, our sacred mischief, and our innocence. May the vulnerabilities that we witnessed in one another as children be protected in adulthood. Keep our storytelling honest as we navigate the reflecting that occurs with time and age. Help us to remember that each of us has our own experience within the family system, that no two understandings of the family are alike, nor do we need to force our apprehension of the family or our parents on one another. Keep us from washing over the harm we may have caused one another in our youth. Help those of us who perpetrated alienation or trauma reckon with it truthfully for our own sakes and for the sake of our siblings. Remind us that apology and forgiveness, however delayed, are not futile. Show us what else love can look like as we age and meet one another for who we are, not who we are assumed to be. *Amen.*

FOR ROMANCE

God of love,

Thank you for creating us to be held by each other—for being a God who does not place power or intellect or even strength at the center of your selfhood, but love. Show us the many faces of love, including romance. Inspire new stories that imagine romance not as a tool for control or manipulation, but as a dance that liberates us in our bodies. Make ours a love containing all magic and mystery. Too often we are so desperate to be loved that it is not the person we fall in love with, but a feeling. Reorient us toward the person, not as object but as a complicated human with their own desires, fears, and needs. Help us keep our love near to wonder, attention, and truth-telling. Protect us from all scrutiny of queer love, allowing us to bear witness to the many ways nonnormative love expands our collective sense of belonging. Have mercy on those who will not encounter romantic love, whatever the reason may be. Remind them that love cannot be reduced to romance or sex. Grant courage to those who desire love but are terrified of it—those who have been hurt or fear getting hurt so much that they run from romance when it finds them. Steady them in your presence, that they would locate the courage to face love when it is safe and good and desired. *Amen.*

FOR WHEN YOU LONG TO BE CHOSEN

God who chooses us,
The pain of feeling unwanted weighs on me. I want to be desired— to know that they think of me before they fall asleep. That they watch me and are waiting too. Help me to grieve the pain of being overlooked, of waiting for something that never comes. In my grief, protect those insecurities that gnaw at me in the wake of rejection. I confess that at times I allow my insecurities and unmet desires to become my deepest motivators. Parse out in me healthy desire from the poisonous ideals of a culture of abuse and narcissistic storytelling. Heal whatever formed me to believe that the only people worth wanting are the ones who don't want me back. Show me the beauty of true reciprocity. Expand my imagination for fulfillment, flourishing, and belonging, that when I am not chosen by who I desire, I would glimpse what love is already tangible to me. And as I honor my waiting, build up my sense of self, that I would no longer submit myself to shape-shifting to be loved in return. In all seasons,

may I recall my own agency; that I have just as much voice and power to be an active participant in pursuing love. I can choose, and there is beauty in that. *Amen.*

FOR PLEASURE

God of desire,
We have become ill-attuned to pleasure in our bodies. We live closer to numbness than sensuality. Reveal the diverse landscape of delight and joy, spreading our search to new places and experiences, to food and sex. Untangle the ways we have conjoined pleasure to things that destroy—abuse, humiliation, bullying, self-harm. We have learned to be ashamed of what brings us pleasure, even learning to cringe at the word itself. Heal those of us who have been taught to ridicule and shame our own bodies—the way we dress, the arousal we feel, the way our bodies appear. Heal those who have been damaged by the menacing voice of purity culture. Free us from the lie that we are dirty or depraved in the absence of actual harm. Deliver us into relationships and communities where pleasure in all its forms is viewed not as a reward, but a beauty that all can access. Liberate us from spiritual teachings that tell us we must submit ourselves to constant suffering to be near to God. Show us God at the table. A God who hungers, craves, admires, and delights. A God who spews the blandness from their mouth. We know how goodness tastes. May we find it. *Amen.*

FOR FRIENDSHIP

Divine Companion,
You are a God who rejects self-sufficiency even in your own personhood. That you exist in a multitude—in sacred community not only with the cosmos but also within yourself—is a mystery to us. Heal the exclusion and alienation of our past through new communities of belonging. We recognize the idol of self-reliance has cast a long shadow over our ability to connect and be together with others.

Show us the tender places in us that are afraid to belong, and make us honest about our desires for nearness. Convict us of our own self-absorption when we begin to view others through their usefulness to us. Show us the joy of witnessing the life of another. Make us responsible and shrewd when we consider our companions. Expose those relationships that are not friendship but predator and prey. Be near to those who long for fun and empowering and deep friendships. Remind us that the depth of disclosure must always revere time, that we would not rush our friends to places where it is not yet safe to go. Help us to delight in every season of friendship and find love in unexpected places. It is scary to belong to each other, but grant us courage to commit ourselves to friendship in a lonely world. *Amen.*

FOR LOVING THE SELF

God of self-embrace,
Show us how you love yourself. Teach us to be present enough to the miracle of us that we could name it without deprecation. For so long we have shrunk ourselves and shape-shifted to stand in crowded rooms. We have learned to be present but not to take up space. To speak but only when spoken to. Protect us from self-hatred, and so too protect us from the guilt we feel when we are unable to muster love for ourselves. Help us to remember that we have survived years under those who made us question our own faces, our own dignity and beauty. We have had our bodies torn from us, evaluated by rubrics of whiteness and thinness. We have had our personalities analyzed and critiqued, showing us at every turn how we can be "better" or "wiser" or "funnier." Let us be proud that we are even praying these words right now. That we refuse to be held captive to the self-hatred this world feeds in us. That we will nourish love and gentleness and creativity, and at last expand. We claim healing. We claim love. We are beautiful. Keep us from shrinking from it. *Amen.*

Breathe

INHALE: Gratitude be my guide.
EXHALE: Love be my breath.

INHALE: I wasn't made to be perfect.
EXHALE: I was made to be loved.

INHALE: I'm no burden.
EXHALE: I am gift.

Confession

Caring God,
We confess that we have not loved this world well. We have not loved ourselves. We have dismissed concepts of love as frivolous and naïve, failing to recognize the wisdom in choosing tenderness and attachment in a society that trains us to exploit one another. We have lost our passions, allowing our days to be consumed with the practical and boring. Our delight has been drained as we try to survive exhaustion. We confess we are afraid, lacking the courage to risk ourselves on love for fear of losing it. We have taken advantage of those we know will not leave us, withholding affection and allowing them to receive so much more of our hatred than our gratitude. Forgive us. And have mercy on all our charades of heartlessness, that we would claim a life of more than mere survival. That we would love and be loved in return, all our days, in love's many forms. *Amen.*

Forgiveness

Let your soul receive this rest: Forgive yourself, choosing self-compassion over unlove. Be assured by the divine that, despite your deepest doubts, you are lovable. That you are adored by God, as they look upon your face and swell with delight. May you be forgiven for how you've replicated lovelessness in the world. And as you are nourished by abounding mercy, may you also extend it, remembering that we are healed by both love received and love given. *Amen.*

Benediction

Now may you dig through the ashes of life and emerge with something beautiful. May you become love and possess the courage to receive it. May you hold and be held, allowing the vulnerable places in you to find company for the journey. *Amen.*

Contemplation

1. How was love demonstrated in your home when you were growing up? How has this formed you, either in resistance to or in alignment with those early experiences?
2. Explore a time when your love was not reciprocated. What did that rejection or fear of rejection bring out in you?
3. What is your deepest love in this season?
4. How do you distinguish the way you love those you know and those you don't know? Become curious about any distinctions.
5. Who do you feel most loved by in this season? How do they translate their love to you in a way that you can receive it?

2 0

MEMORY

*To accept one's past—one's history—is not the same thing
as drowning in it; it is learning how to use it. An invented
past can never be used; it cracks and crumbles under the
pressures of life like clay in a season of drought.*

—JAMES BALDWIN

*I am not a historian. I happen to think that the content of
my mother's life—her myths, her superstitions, her prayers,
the contents of her pantry, the smell of her kitchen, the
song that escaped from her sometimes parched lips, her
thoughtful repose and pregnant laughter—are all worthy
of art.*

—AUGUST WILSON

LETTER XX | TO THE KEEPERS OF STORIES

People in my family struggle with their memory. Moments only
visit us; they tend not to remain.

I find it remarkable when people recount stories from when they
were as young as three years old. Memories of my childhood are
sparse. Trauma takes a toll on the memory, for better or worse. Not
all moments were *meant* to be recalled. The body spares us in ways
the world cannot. But in protecting me from the terrible memories,
it has also placed a fog over the beautiful ones.

A handful of years ago, I was kneeling in a room filled with old
books and diaries, trinkets and artifacts passed down through generations in my husband's family, and suddenly I was filled with a jealous
and unexpected grief. My family had no journals, no real artifacts
that had been preserved. Some of this, to be sure, had been stolen
from us when my ancestors were abducted and sold into slavery. In-

heritances are hard to pass down when one's wrists are in chains. But much of our family story, even in recent generations, has also been marked by poverty. I suspect my gramma and great-grandpa and others didn't believe they had anything *worth* passing on.

When my gramma passed, I snuck into her room and buried myself under her covers, letting the scent of Shalimar perfume hold me. After a while, I couldn't smell her anymore. It was now my own smell that haunted me. When I emerged from the bed, my sister was there too, looking through my gramma's jewelry box, a few rusted rings and some costume jewelry. Nothing lasting. We had come for the same thing, something to remember her by. Something capable of holding the memory of her. Our minds alone could not be trusted.

My sister thumbed the pillowcase next to me. *At least you have her stories . . .* I had been interviewing different family members for a few years, and in the year before her death, had been calling my gramma weekly to draw out the details of her life. I recorded her so that my kids and their kids, if they have them, will not just read her words but also be able to hear the smooth velvet of her voice. Every pause, every sigh. Some of those stories are preserved in my first book—an artifact of both liberation and grief.

My gramma's stories did not always rest easy on the bones. I met her in ways I never thought I would. I met memories of both dignity and trauma. Sorrow and survival that didn't originate with me but was inherited in my body. A story that doesn't resolve. But it is ours.

In a country that is so staunchly delusional about its own history, so committed to a collective amnesia, it is a feat to remember rightly. Maybe you've known how it feels to have someone rewrite history or make you question your own memory. You know the danger of the oppressor turned historian. Of countries that have buried corpses in unmarked graves, hoping no one would ever uncover what lies beneath. That our memory has survived at all is a miracle. Remembering is no small act of defiance. My gramma knew pain, as her mother did, and her mother's mother. But whatever integrity and beauty lived in them survives in me.

Toni Morrison compared memory to the Mississippi River, which had been redirected and straightened out by humans to make room for houses and carriages, but still floods the places it once was.

"Floods" is the word they use, but in fact it is not flooding; it is remembering. Remembering where it used to be. All water has a perfect memory and is forever trying to get back to where it was. Writers are like that: remembering where we were, what valley we ran through, what the banks were like, the light that was there and the route back to our original place.

I'm learning to follow the water—to take the time to retrace and reclaim what once was. Not just for my own sense of self—though this is part of it—but because I'm not convinced we will survive without habits of remembrance. Where our individual memory wanes, collective memory must be our flood.

It's been a year and a half since my gramma passed on. A small translucent jar of Shalimar powder rests on my nightstand. At night, I dust my pillow with it and pray to meet her in my dreams. In the daytime, I'm starting to smell like her.

Keep memory,
C

remains

The blue residue on your fingers that you called
Hypothermia felt warm on my skin.

Your teeth were like those pebbles we would collect in the alley
And pretend were ancient jewels.

I remember every song you ever played me and the way
Your face looked waiting
as I listened.

The glass of water spilled over the canvas and we watched the
paint blur;
The waves losing their outline made them look more real.

This, I remember—

Chess at midnight
Baldwin at sunrise
Getting syrup in your eyes and
offering you my tongue.
The first time you called me by my full name.
The last time you called me by my full name.
Limping home after you promised me
You'd never try again.

You took everything with you
Including me.

Prayers

FOR COLLECTIVE REMEMBRANCE

God who remembers,
We are grateful for all the ways this world echoes with memory—ancient etches in stone, gorges carrying the shape of water. Make us people of deep remembrance. In a world that would be content to have us forget our own names, keep them on our tongue. Keep our mother's and grandmothers' and great-grandmothers' names near to us; not that we would idealize them but that we would practice an abiding reverence for all that has formed us. Awaken our families to the necessity of story exchange. May we learn how to both recount memories and receive them with a dignity worthy of its subjects. When the familial memory is challenged, may we humble ourselves to the challenger, always being willing to turn the same memory over in a new palm; and in holding it, become more whole. When our own memory wanes, may you provide people who can carry our memories for us. Send us to the far places in ourselves, to our child selves, that we could practice compassion where it was not, kindness where it was absent, and find some manner of healing through the portal that is memory. *Ase.*

FOR WHEN SOMEONE GASLIGHTS YOU

Honest God,
It is taxing having to prove our own stories. We know. We know what happened, what was said or done or not done. But our memories have endured so much critique and accusation that we are beginning to question ourselves. Affirm our memory as sacred. Teach us to recognize when we are not misremembering, only being manipulated into self-doubt. Train us to perceive these moments when someone would rather have us insecure in our own mind than take responsibility for

the truth of an encounter. Expose this, that they would never again be believed by the vulnerable. Ground us in self-belief, not that our own recollection would never be questioned, but that it would be honored with compassion and honesty, never as an attempt to achieve a particular outcome or protect those who have done harm. We know; help us honor our knowing. We remember and tell it. *Amen.*

FOR THOSE THINGS OUR MINDS SHIELD US FROM

God who protects,

Thank you for granting our bodies the wisdom to know when to protect us from our own memory. That we cannot relive every moment of our lives is a mercy we do not readily comprehend. Keep us from traveling into memories that will bring more traumatization than liberation. Protect us from making a home out of memories that are cruel and unloving; not that we would dismiss the past as inconsequential, but that we would not be held captive by it in detail. Help us to learn how to honor our stories while still implementing boundaries for our own welfare. Guide us as we discern which memories are safe to travel into, and on the journeys we dare to take, let us go with trusted companions—that we would never become too disoriented to find our way back to center. Help us to grieve every unnamed or forgotten moment, every beautiful memory that was stolen as collateral damage. And be with us in our bodies as emotions stir what we don't have language for. May we rest in you and meet our bodies with compassion. *Amen.*

FOR GRIEVING WHAT WILL BE FORGOTTEN

God of forgotten things,

We grieve what has been lost to time. Be near to us as we lament those moments or stories that it seems may never return to us. Help us to be gentle with ourselves in our forgetting. Keep us from punishing or turning against our own minds as we age, that we would remember there is something uniquely sacred about those stories that we can never revisit but that live in us nonetheless. Help us to hold fast to what memories we can, and release what can be held no longer. May it be a sacred release, honoring our own limitations and the beauty of stories that don't need to be clear in order to be meaningful. Grant us compassion for the sick and all those who are struggling to remember even the faces of those they love. Give us the wisdom and the tenderness to hold their memory for them, that when they need a fragment of it, we might place it gently in their hands if only for a little while. Remind us that our remembrance is no less beautiful. May time be not a thief but a friend to us. *Amen.*

FOR WHEN HISTORY MISREMEMBERS

God who reclaims,
It's chilling to watch those in power rewrite history again and again. We are haunted by every true memory killed and buried by those who would be implicated. Help us to remember that the oppressor can never be trusted as historian. Let us resist. Remind us of the power in collective memory, that our path to justice requires a fierce commitment to shared story. Reclaim the history books that contain lies and propaganda—those lessons that only serve to wash the blood from our own hands before anyone can bear witness to it. Expose the unflinching erasure of Indigenous story, of Black story, of queer story, and protect us as we try to resurrect the truth. Raise up new historians, people capable of nuance and complexity. People who refuse to look away from horror, and who document the truth even to their own detriment. We will not submit to the collective delusion that hovers around us. May collective memory get us free. May false memory die in the presence of those who remember. *Amen.*

FOR THE ANCESTORS

To acknowledge our ancestors means we are aware that we did not make ourselves, that the line stretches all the way back, perhaps, to God; or to Gods. We remember them because it is an easy thing to forget: that we are not the first to suffer, rebel, fight, love and die. The grace with which we embrace life, in spite of the pain, the sorrows, is always a measure of what has gone before.

—Alice Walker

God our ancestor,

We give thanks that you are a God who does not sever us from our ancestors but continually calls us toward habits of remembrance. That you make space to name lineages throughout sacred texts is an invitation to honor story as it stretches across time and space. Free us from oppressive spiritual teachings that alienate us from our ancestors. Let us embrace a spirituality that names and honors those mystical members of the divine community who have been lost to death. Let us remember those whose bodies endured the deepest evils, that we might ground ourselves in our own bodies, and in doing so find our belief more whole. Let us remember those who preserved our deepest joy, that we might realize we've inherited far more than trauma. Remind us that those excluded in life will not be excluded in death. Our saints belong and are worthy of honor. *Amen.*

Breathe

INHALE: God, protect our stories.
EXHALE: Make us keepers of our memory.

INHALE: I come from pain.
EXHALE: I come from beauty.

INHALE: I will not protect the lie.
EXHALE: I remember.

Confession

Present God,

We confess that we have not cared well for our memory, personal and collective. We occupy ourselves with dreaming of the future and dismiss habits of remembrance and of honoring the past. We have let our stories die without compassion or reverence. We have not become curious about our elders and ancestors. Forgive us and have mercy on us, that we would encounter our own souls with greater clarity through the stories that formed us. Ground us, that our memories would not be a torment to us, but would remind us that we will endure. Help us to grieve, to excavate both pain and beauty without being destroyed. And if we dream for what's to come, may it be a dream that holds memory for all that has made us. *Amen.*

Forgiveness

Let your soul receive this rest: The God who keeps record can forgive you for how you've stewarded yours. May they have mercy on all the memories that have been lost, stolen, or colonized. Receive healing and shelter from that which is too much to bear, that you would learn forgetting is sometimes a mercy of its own kind. Forgive yourself, claiming and preserving many stories, and honoring collective memory as the lifeblood of our liberation. *Amen.*

Benediction

May the Sacred Chronicler travel with you into the stories that have formed you, that having made that pilgrimage, you would return freer and more whole, body and soul. *Amen.*

Contemplation

1. What practices of remembrance do you honor throughout the year?
2. What does storytelling look like in your family? Is there one trusted "historian"? Can the members of your family be trusted to carry memory?

3. Travel into a memory of feeling deep belief in yourself. Where do you feel that self-belief in your body?

4. Explore a time when your recollection of an event or a circumstance was questioned. How do you protect the story as you lived it while remaining open to shared memory?

5. What is one story your country believes about itself that is a false memory? How do you resist this?

21

MORTALITY

Life is tragic simply because the earth turns and the sun inexorably rises and sets, and one day, for each of us, the sun will go down for the last, last time. Perhaps the whole root of our trouble, the human trouble, is that we will sacrifice all the beauty of our lives, will imprison ourselves in totems, taboos, crosses, blood sacrifices, steeples, mosques, races, armies, flags, nations, in order to deny the fact of death, which is the only fact we have.

—JAMES BALDWIN

They held hands and knew that only the coffin would lie in the earth; the bubbly laughter and the press of fingers in the palm would stay aboveground forever. At first, as they stood there, their hands were clenched together. They relaxed slowly until during the walk back home their fingers were laced in as gentle a clasp as that of any two young girlfriends trotting up the road on a summer day wondering what happened to butterflies in the winter.

—TONI MORRISON

LETTER XXI | TO MORTAL SOULS

When did you first know about death? That not everything that's loved remains? If there was a singular moment when I first became aware of my own mortality, I cannot recall it. I remember the first funeral I attended—the first time death got close enough to mean something. But learning about my own temporality? It was unremarkable.

What does it mean that the day we discover death itself is immemorable to most of us? Are we in denial from the start, learning to look away from this shared fate?

A few years back, I read about the Toraja people of Indonesia who have unique rituals around the dead. When someone dies, it can take years to bury them. They'll clothe them, speak to them, include them in the land of the living. Some perform a sacred ritual called *ma'nene'* yearly, in which they unbury the dead, hold them, clean them, and spend time with them. I watched videos of kids digging tiny hands into open coffins, photos of corpses with cigarettes hanging freely in their mouths, soda and meals laid at their feet.

As someone accustomed to Western rituals of death and dying, I had to resist much of my instincts toward judgment, confronting the ways I mistake my own understanding of death as innately superior. When I did so and listened to local Torajans explain their customs, I came to find a certain beauty in it.

What does it mean to be a people surrounded by death yet not plagued by it? To attune oneself to mortality without being frightened? The Toraja do not rush their dead belowground. They are capable of bearing witness to the grotesque in death—grieving deeply but honoring mortality nonetheless. This ritual of unearthing what has died and staring decay in the face is forming them, forming their children.

When I became sick, I began to think about my death often. When you don't know what is happening to your body, it's difficult not to imagine its end. I'm telling you this now, but I don't tell those close to me. In some ways they are more afraid than I am. But I think the only way I could survive without being tormented by what was to come was to become painfully familiar with my own mortality. It's a very complicated thing to explain to someone. That the more I accepted that I would die, the easier it would be to live.

But I should tell you, accepting that you will die and being unafraid to die are two very different things. Mortality, as many have argued, is the great human equalizer. It is the one certainty that no human will escape. This would be more comforting if not for the fact that what meets us after our dying remains not just opaque, but inconceivable. Religions throughout history have gone to great lengths to convince themselves that the unknown of death is knowable. We've embraced elaborate stories and images that will never not be beautiful to me. But they are hardly incontestable.

August Wilson's play, *Fences*, takes place in the neighborhood where my mother lived. Throughout the play, the character Troy is visited by Death personified. Having survived the brink of death once before, he says:

> Death ain't nothing. I done seen him. Done wrassled with him. You can't tell me nothing about death. Death ain't nothing but a fastball on the outside corner. And you know what I'll do to that! Lookee here, Bono . . . am I lying? You get one of them fastballs, about waist high, over the outside corner of the plate where you can get the meat of the bat on it . . . and good god! You can kiss it goodbye. Now, am I lying?

Troy is a near-perfect emblem of both the mentality that death is something to be beaten, and the feigned invincibility that many men choose when they are too terrified to contend with the inevitable. But I say "near-perfect," because at other times it seems like he is willing to concede. He says, "Alright . . . Mr. Death. . . . I'm gonna take and build me a fence around this yard. See? I'm gonna build me a fence around what belongs to me. And then I want you to stay on the other side. See? You stay over there until you're ready for me." There's a negotiation with his own mortality. *Until you're ready for me.* However large, however resilient, each of us knows we are no God. As a Black man living in Pittsburgh in the middle of the civil rights movement, Troy, for all his bravado, would have been strikingly aware of his own mortality. He may be deluded, but it is not born of naïveté.

I cannot write to you in good faith claiming beauty in death without honoring that death also steals something from us. To lose someone is to lose a world. Everything that remains in their absence so too is altered. The familiar becomes strange. Even those who are ready to pass may still weep at death's door. Death hurts. We don't have to pretend otherwise. We can hold space for the tragedy of mortality alongside its beauty.

You can build a hundred fences, but death obeys no boundary lines. The fence, as it were, only succeeds in holding you. I'm not telling you not to grieve, not to curse the sky in the absence of the one you've lost. I'm telling you not everything needs to last for it to be beautiful. That there is a certain mystery suspended between my heart and yours. The blood will stop. Fence or no fence, whether we look or fail to look. Death doesn't always need to be a haunting. There is beauty in impermanence, a rest that comes for all of us. If you're a ghost, I'm a ghost.

Still breathing,
C

soundlessness

this time I'm going out like my momma
who pulled her pantyhose up with bright
blue nails without ever piercing
the mesh
a thin line
of smoke dangling from her mouth
like the end of an exorcism

I told you everything you need to know about
ashes and how to wash
the smell from the sofa
when you were supposed to be sleeping
and not
watching like a ghost
as she falls through the house
hands cradling her own
neck like a newborn

A door opens.

and when the goddess of her
visits
your bedside smoking
mouth opening but no sound
releasing
know the void is not a curse

this time I'm going
out to where the frogs hide

croaking invisible
while the hairs
rise from my neck
this haunting lullaby
this beautiful, uncertain song

Prayers

FOR THE DEATH OF A CHILD

God of the void,

I don't know how to go on. This void is cruel and relentless, and I don't want to figure out how to exist with it haunting every room I enter. And I blame you. I won't apologize for that. But if you're real, have mercy on me. Hold me up because I can't. Or lay me down to sleep so I can wake up from the nightmare of emptiness. I know I'll never be myself again, but whoever this is—this hidden grief that now occupies my selfhood—help me to meet them. I'm a stranger to myself. Ground me. Steady me. And whatever mystery the one I love met on the other side of breathing, let it be kind and safe and loving. *Amen.*

FOR AGING

God of old,

Some days it's as if the world is looking right through us. Comfort us as we are bombarded with a hundred tiny reminders that to some we matter less and less. In a world that devalues and discards the elderly, make our dignity known. We have been cast to the margins of society's most pressing conversations. We have been forgotten by family and friends. Help us to possess a stability of heart as we are forced to question our worth and contribution daily. Protect us from the ageism of a culture that fetishizes youth. They want every trace of our days erased from our flesh, our skin, our hair. Reveal the toxic irony of this, for it is in the days that we've lived that we have become more human. Each year that passes brings us closer in alignment with our true selves. May we know our own interior landscapes by heart, that we would be familiar enough with our own thoughts, fears, and loves to find rest with ourselves.

Grant us imagination for new ways of existing in the world, that we would not be confined by time's expectations, but would retain a sacred vigor for life in the company of those who love us. We have lived. Give us the wisdom to make sense of our days. This body has carried us. Give us courage to honor it, as we meet it anew each day. *Amen.*

FOR GRIEVING A DEATH

God who cried,
We are grateful that you are well acquainted with grief. That you make space for our deepest sorrows is a tender offering in this season. Show us how to mourn. Show us how to weep, and curse, and remember well the one who has departed. Make our grieving honest, that we would never feel as if we must force sorrow for our love to be real. Help us to weep when we need, and laugh when we need, showing great patience for our interior intricacies. We understand that death visits each of us. But this feels cruel and disorienting, like we've been ripped from what we've known life to be and thrust into this hollow space that feels unfillable. Comfort those for whom death has come too soon. Show us who we are in their absence, what breathing feels like with less air in the room. And have mercy on the dead and dying, that they would be able to grieve for themselves—that they could honor their own loss and meet death settled in themselves, with an inner calm that is prepared to encounter the uncharted. May the unknowable be kind and healing and liberating to this person whom we have loved. *Amen.*

FOR GRIEVING SOMEONE WHO DIDN'T LOVE YOU WELL

God of complicated grief,
I don't know how to feel. I only know what I am supposed to feel, which is daunting, suffocating. Stay close as I struggle to grasp my

own grief. Help me to make peace with a kind of mourning that is nuanced and distinct. Keep me from idealizing or demonizing the relationship in death, and help me be present to the complexities of a person who didn't love me well. Protect me from guilt as I become honest about how I feel. When it's sorrow, let it be a sorrow that is free; knowing that I was able to love an imperfect human. When it's relief, let it be a relief that is unashamed of itself; knowing that I deserved better than what this person was able to give me. And if I feel nothing at all, may it be a nothingness that is aware of all the emotions already spent. May the nothingness not be numbness but a mercy. The mercy of peace in a season of profound loss. I don't know what I'll feel tomorrow or how sorrow will settle in the years to come, but help me make space for grief's many faces. I can feel more than one thing. *May it be so.*

FOR THE THINGS THAT DIE IN US WHILE WE'RE STILL ALIVE

God of dead dreams,

Help us to hold space for all that dies in us while we're still alive. We have had passions depart from us unannounced, hopes extinguished without warning. Show us who we are in the absence of those loves. Help us to discern when the passion has died for our own becoming, and when it should be resurrected. We confess that we have let the innocence of our wonder die. We have emptied ourselves of our child selves, forgetting what it means to delight and forgive and be curious. Protect us from the terrible fate of the cynic. Help us to grieve what's lost, mourning the dreams that will never come to pass, even those that still stir and ache in us. Show us how to exist when we know all that we want will not be realized. Keep us from being rushed from the grief of a dying dream. May we know that its withholding is not a punishment nor indicative of our own worth, and that we can be grateful for what is while honoring the pain of what will never be. *Amen.*

FOR THE BEAUTY IN IMPERMANENCE

God of the unlasting,
We have been trained to believe that the beautiful things are the things that last. Help us to hold this truth in harmony with the knowledge that there is also a mysterious beauty in what does not remain. We have clung to that which is static and unchanging, defining the divine as changeless when you are also fluid and expansive, constant in your remaking of us. Protect us from the lie that death is only ever tragedy. Remind us that not all things were meant to last. Remind us that the beauty of autumn is in its temporality— that if the leaves were always red, they'd fail to stir us at all. Give us a reverence for the things that rust. That the things that decay become the dirt that sustains us. As we submit to time, not as thief but as artist, may we apprehend the beauty of fleeting things. Every sunset, every first dance, the emptied beehive. Help us to make space for the grief of all that doesn't last, while still honoring the liberation of all that refuses to stay. If only for a moment, there is beauty. We will pause for it. *Amen.*

Breathe

INHALE: This breath will end.
EXHALE: There is beauty in impermanence.

INHALE: God, I am scared.
EXHALE: Meet this fear with peace.

INHALE: Every breath will rest.
EXHALE: Prepare us for mystery.

Confession

Divine Maker,
We confess that we have not always lived the way we wanted. We have not always honored ourselves, the land, or the people whose

weight it bears. There are days we believed in our own invincibility, shrinking from the frailty of life. Days when we have taken for granted all that is good and true and beautiful in this life. We are truly sorry, and we ask forgiveness—from you, from the world, and from ourselves. Our lives have been held together by every mundane mercy. We claim this grace, forgiving ourselves, and believing in our souls that we have done what we could to be human and whole in this world. *Amen.*

Forgiveness

Let your soul receive this rest: The God who made even the stars mortal sends the light of you to visit those who remain. As you look into the sacred dark of death, unknowable and opaque, may the mystery of what is to come be a comfort and not a terror. And as you feel the forgiveness of the divine cover you—for any harm, for anything left undone in this life—may God call to mind the beauty and wonder that you've offered this world. May you feel your soul now put at peace, in sacred harmony with the cosmos. Inhale. Exhale. As you enter a sacred and abiding rest. May mystery be your home now and forever. *Amen.*

Benediction

May you depart in peace, with reverence for the body—however frail. With compassion for your interior life—however complicated. And with surviving memory for all the days of your mortal soul. *Amen.*

Contemplation

1. What emotions come to you when you think about your own mortality?
2. What stories of an afterlife have formed you? How do they comfort you? How do they scare you?

3. Explore any stories of being near to someone who is dying. How did bearing witness to someone passing change you?
4. Is legacy important to you? Why or why not?
5. How do you think about aging bodies? Become honest about any shame, grief, or loss that you are already experiencing in your body.

Part Two
By Time

1

DAWN

A LITURGY FOR MORNING PRAYER

The guide opens this liturgy by reading a quotation from the ancestors, followed by one or more of the invitation verses.

Words in bold can be recited in unison by a collective

Ancestors

> I'm a black ocean, leaping and wide,
> Welling and swelling I bear in the tide.
>
> Leaving behind nights of terror and fear
> I rise
> Into a daybreak that's wondrously clear
>
> —Maya Angelou

Invitation

> I rise before dawn and cry for help;
> I put my hope in your words.
>
> —Psalm 119:147 (NRSVA)

"I have indeed seen the misery of my people in Egypt. I have heard them crying out because of their slave drivers, and I am concerned about their suffering. So I have come down to rescue them . . . and to bring them up out of that land into a good and spacious land, a land flowing with milk and honey."

> —Exodus 3:7–8 (NIV)

Confession

The guide speaks to the collective

Sacred companions,
We begin this day near to the divine, near to our ancestors, and near to our own souls. In the company of the collective, we ground our day in truth-telling, compassion, and the mystery of our humanity. As we speak these words, may we be granted the courage required for interior honesty, the self-possession required to remain in our bodies, and a renewed belief in our liberation.

Together we listen to our own interior worlds for the ways in which we've contributed to bondage and decay—in the world, in others, and in ourselves.

Silence may be kept

In unison

Forgiving God,
Make us human. We confess all the ways we have suppressed dignity and limited liberation. We have not pursued justice and reparation for the historically excluded and oppressed. We have neglected and dismissed those with less power than us—Black souls, queer souls, trans souls. We have not loved the bodies of the disabled nor the minds of the neurodivergent. Our children and elders, we have not taken seriously as fellow humans. We have not comforted the lonely or outcast. We are deeply sorry, our souls troubled in the absence of forgiveness and repair. Examine our hearts, and where you find true repentance, grant us pardon. Examine our lives, and where full reparation has been made, grant us mercy. Forgive us, God, that in your abiding kindness we would be restored to deeper forms of humanity for the good of the cosmos. *Amen.*

Forgiveness

The guide speaks over the collective

Let your soul receive this rest: The divine comforter comforts us now. May we be freed from the addiction of toxic individualism, that we would know a life lived within the dignity of the collective. May we be forgiven and unchained from the altars of capitalism and elitism. As we confront every habit of exclusion and neglect, every alienation and deprivation, may our forgiveness be made real to us. And as we journey through this day, may we look up and be reminded that we have a responsibility to each face we encounter. That our freedom, our humanity, depends on this. Now feel the tenderness of divine mercy pass through us and keep us. May it rise in us and alchemize into self-forgiveness, a sacred entrance to enduring change. *Amen.*

Daily Prayer

In unison

God our maker,
We honor the sacred multitude that resides in you.
May the guardian in you protect us.
May the child in you delight in us.
May the friend in you challenge us.
May your ashes resurrect us.
May your sky shelter us.
May the mystery of you liberate us.
Provide abundance and healing in all forms to those who need it
    today,
And deliver us from shame, hatred, and the chains that bind us.
For you have made us—*glory*—and we are still being made.
    Amen.

Words in bold can be recited in unison by a collective

But I will sing of your strength,
in the morning I will sing of your love;
for you are my fortress,
my refuge in times of trouble.

You are my strength,
I sing praise to you;
you, God, are my fortress,
my God on whom I can rely.

—Psalm 59:16–17 (NIV)

Those who are able can rise or may assume a different posture

Glory to God, who came in flesh, for all flesh.

Praise the One Who Frees.
We are free indeed.

Wisdom

"Even if you are not ready for day
it cannot always be night."

—Gwendolyn Brooks

First Reading | Listening

Alternate passages from sacred literature may be read

Does not wisdom call,
and does not understanding raise her voice?
On the heights, beside the way,
at the crossroads she takes her stand;
beside the gates in front of the town,
at the entrance of the portals she cries out:
'To you, O people, I call,
and my cry is to all that live.

O simple ones, learn prudence;
  acquire intelligence, you who lack it.
Hear, for I will speak noble things,
  and from my lips will come what is right;
for my mouth will utter truth;
  wickedness is an abomination to my lips.
All the words of my mouth are righteous;
  there is nothing twisted or crooked in them.
They are all straight to one who understands
  and right to those who find knowledge.
Take my instruction instead of silver,
  and knowledge rather than choice gold;
for wisdom is better than jewels,
  and all that you may desire cannot compare with her.
I, wisdom, live with prudence,
  and I attain knowledge and discretion.
The fear of the LORD is hatred of evil.
  . . .
I walk in the way of righteousness,
  along the paths of justice,
endowing with wealth those who love me,
  and filling their treasuries.
The LORD created me at the beginning of his work,
  the first of his acts of long ago.
Ages ago I was set up,
  at the first, before the beginning of the earth.
When there were no depths I was brought forth,
  when there were no springs abounding with water.
Before the mountains had been shaped,
  before the hills, I was brought forth—
when he had not yet made earth and fields,
  or the world's first bits of soil.
When he established the heavens, I was there,
  when he drew a circle on the face of the deep,

when he made firm the skies above,
  when he established the fountains of the deep,
when he assigned to the sea its limit,
  so that the waters might not transgress his command,
when he marked out the foundations of the earth.'

—Proverbs 8:1–13, 20–29 (NRSVA)

Second Reading | In the Silence

Alternate passages from sacred literature may be read

Then [Elijah] was afraid; he got up and fled for his life, and came to Beer-sheba, which belongs to Judah; he left his servant there.

But he himself went a day's journey into the wilderness, and came and sat down under a solitary broom tree. He asked that he might die: 'It is enough; now, O LORD, take away my life, for I am no better than my ancestors.' Then he lay down under the broom tree and fell asleep. Suddenly an angel touched him and said to him, 'Get up and eat.' He looked, and there at his head was a cake baked on hot stones, and a jar of water. He ate and drank, and lay down again. The angel of the LORD came a second time, touched him, and said, 'Get up and eat, otherwise the journey will be too much for you.' He got up, and ate and drank; then he went in the strength of that food for forty days and forty nights to Horeb the mount of God. At that place he came to a cave, and spent the night there.

Then the word of the LORD came to him, saying, 'What are you doing here, Elijah?' He answered, 'I have been very zealous for the LORD, the God of hosts; for the Israelites have forsaken your covenant, thrown down your altars, and killed your prophets with the sword. I alone am left, and they are seeking my life, to take it away.'

He said, 'Go out and stand on the mountain before the LORD, for the LORD is about to pass by.' Now there was a great wind, so strong that it was splitting mountains and breaking rocks in pieces before the LORD, but the LORD was not in the wind; and after the wind an earthquake, but the LORD was not in the earthquake; and after the earthquake a fire, but the LORD was not in the fire; and after the fire a sound of sheer silence. When Elijah heard it, he wrapped his face in his mantle and went out and stood at the entrance of the cave. Then there came a voice to him that said, 'What are you doing here, Elijah?'

—1 Kings 19:3–13 (NRSVA)

Silence

In the stillness of the quiet, if we listen,
We can hear the whisper in the heart
Giving strength to weakness, courage to fear, hope to despair.

—Howard Thurman

The LORD is in his holy temple;
let all the earth keep silence before him.

—Habakkuk 2:20 (NRSVA)

Silence kept (two to five minutes)

Psalm Reading

Can be replaced with a different psalm, song, or poem

Words in bold can be recited in unison by a collective

O LORD, my heart is not lifted up,
my eyes are not raised too high;
I do not occupy myself with things
too great and too marvellous for me.
But I have calmed and quieted my soul,
like a weaned child with its mother;
my soul is like the weaned child that is with me.
O Israel, hope in the LORD
from this time on and for evermore.

—Psalm 131:1–3 (NRSVA)

Prayers of the People

Words in bold can be recited in unison by a collective

Wise and Loving Creator, we dare to pray to you this morning with the boldness you have given us in our divine making. We hold space for the sorrows and joys of the world, our community, and every story carried into this space today. After I speak each petition aloud, I will provide pause for silence. Then, ending with the words, "*God, in mystery,*" I invite the collective to respond, "***Listen and have mercy.***"

God of dirt and sky, have mercy on this land. Our greed is a fire, consuming and destroying without concern. Protect the soil from exhaustion and overwork. Protect the waters that run through it from being colonized by our waste. Grant the earth the rest that it has long desired, that star and moon and sea and creature would be brought into shalom again. *God, in mystery*—**Listen and have mercy.**

God who doesn't belong to us, we confess all the ways we believe ourselves to be superior to other nations. Reveal to us our nation's delusions, that we would tell the truth about the blood on our hands, the nooses on our own trees. Guide us in the way of justice and truth, and release us from any pretense of moral authority. May those nations that have been economically excluded and exploited reclaim what is theirs without fear of retribution from the global tyrants. *God, in mystery*—**Listen and have mercy.**

Honest God, whose sensitivity and humility flow through this world, we ask you to renew our country. May the president, governors, and all those who hold office and authority possess the wisdom, competence, and humility to know and to do what's right. May they work with integrity, serving the common good with strategy and prioritizing dignity. Raise up civil servants to organize, petition, march, and bring justice and provision to those in suffering. *God, in mystery*—**Listen and have mercy.**

Tender God, show us what it means to care for children in our midst. Help us to regulate ourselves as we teach them how to be patient discerners of their emotions, needs, and desires. Grant us patience, that we would never be too quick to dismiss their thoughts or questions in arrogance. Expose our desire to control them, to craft them in our own image as opposed to honoring the truth of them. May we submit ourselves to learn from the young—their delight, their curiosity—and through them find ourselves restored to the wonder and joy of our youth. *God, in mystery*—**Listen and have mercy.**

Loving God, who holds together all things, we pray for our immediate community; particularly those in seasons of loneliness, need, or grief. Those suffering from ailing physical or mental health. Would you bring life to our bodies and reveal yourself as near to us. *God, in mystery*—**Listen and have mercy.**

And we pray now for all the cares, concerns, and celebrations alive in this space today—

Pause for those present to speak brief petitions or offer names aloud

God, in mystery—**Listen and have mercy.**

God, hear our prayers, and through mystery and miracle, meet our deepest longings with care and provision, that we may live each day believing in our worth as sacred image bearers of the divine. ***Amen.***

Collect for Dawn

God at dawn,
You have carried us through the long passage of night and into another morning. Awaken us now to today's sacred potential. Grant us imagination for community, wonder, and the kind of work that honors and doesn't degrade us. Place a soothing hand over all who are anxious, that even in the unknown, they would journey into the day grounded and at peace in the arms of the divine. And as we depart from this place, protect each of us as we risk ourselves again on living. Glory to the one who resurrects us daily. *Amen.*

Come, let us honor the one who made us and woke us to meet another morning.

And remain near to our interior worlds as we venture into the day.

Closing

And may the God who spoke day and night, sea and land, dirt and star into being, keep you near to your own dignity today. May the divine call you into your own story, and daily reveal your own face to you—a face worthy, forgiven, beautiful. *Amen.*

ALTERNATE PASSAGES BY CONCERN

Lament—Psalm 42:1–11; Jeremiah 9:17–24; John 11:1–35
Repair—Genesis 11:1–9; Zephaniah 3:9–20; Isaiah 55:1–13
Resistance—Exodus 1:8–20; Judges 4:4–22; Psalm 121
Liberation—Exodus 3:1–17; Isaiah 61:1–11; Psalm 146

DAY

A LITURGY FOR MIDDAY PRAYER

Ancestors

The world is like a Mask dancing. If you want to see it well
you do not stand in one place.

—Chinua Achebe

Invitation

Can be read responsively

The day is long.
God, renew our strength.
Be near to our souls.
Keep us near to ourselves.

First Reading | A Word for Exiles

Alternate passages from sacred literature may be read

This is what the LORD Almighty, the God of Israel, says to all
those I carried into exile from Jerusalem to Babylon: "Build
houses and settle down; plant gardens and eat what they produce. Marry and have sons and daughters; find wives for your
sons and give your daughters in marriage, so that they too may
have sons and daughters. Increase in number there; do not de-
crease. Also, seek the peace and prosperity of the city to which I

have carried you into exile. Pray to the LORD for it, because if it prospers, you too will prosper."

—Jeremiah 29:4–7 (NIV)

Wisdom

I did not tell you that it would be okay, because I have never believed it would be okay. What I told you is what your grandparents tried to tell me: that this is your country, that this is your world, that this is your body, and you must find some way to live within the all of it.

—Ta-Nehisi Coates

Daily Prayer

In unison

God, our maker,
We honor the sacred multitude that resides in you.
May the guardian in you protect us.
May the child in you delight in us.
May the friend in you challenge us.
May your ashes resurrect us.
May your sky shelter us.
May the mystery of you liberate us.
Provide abundance and healing in all forms to those who need it
    today,
And deliver us from shame, hatred, and the chains that bind us.
For you have made us—*glory*—and we are still being made.
    Amen.

Second Reading | *A Sound that Remembers*

Alternate passages from sacred literature may be read

So they gave money to the masons and the carpenters, and food, drink, and oil to the Sidonians and the Tyrians to bring cedar trees from Lebanon to the sea, to Joppa, according to the grant that they had from King Cyrus of Persia.

In the second year after their arrival at the house of God at Jerusalem, in the second month, Zerubbabel son of Shealtiel and Jeshua son of Jozadak made a beginning, together with the rest of their people, the priests and the Levites and all who had come to Jerusalem from the captivity. They appointed the Levites, from twenty years old and upwards, to have the oversight of the work on the house of the LORD. And Jeshua with his sons and his kin, and Kadmiel and his sons, Binnui and Hodaviah along with the sons of Henadad, the Levites, their sons and kin, together took charge of the workers in the house of God.

When the builders laid the foundation of the temple of the LORD, the priests in their vestments were stationed to praise the LORD with trumpets, and the Levites, the sons of Asaph, with cymbals, according to the directions of King David of Israel; and they sang responsively, praising and giving thanks to the LORD,

'For he is good,
for his steadfast love endures for ever towards Israel.'

And all the people responded with a great shout when they praised the LORD, because the foundation of the house of the LORD was laid. But many of the priests and Levites and heads of families, old people who had seen the first house on its foundations, wept with a loud voice when they saw this house, though many shouted aloud for joy, so that the people could not distinguish the sound of the joyful shout from the sound of the people's weeping, for the people shouted so loudly that the sound was heard far away.

—Ezra 3:7–13 (NRSVA)

Praying responsively

Glory to the God who knows us and keeps us.
**Protect our stories—the terrible and the beautiful, the grand
and the mundane.** *Amen.*

Gospel Reading | No Longer Hidden

Alternate passages from sacred literature may be read

> Now there was a woman who had been suffering from
> haemorrhages for twelve years; and though she had spent all
> she had on physicians, no one could cure her. She came up
> behind him and touched the fringe of his clothes, and
> immediately her haemorrhage stopped. Then Jesus asked,
> 'Who touched me?' When all denied it, Peter said, 'Master,
> the crowds surround you and press in on you.' But Jesus said,
> 'Someone touched me; for I noticed that power had gone out
> from me.' When the woman saw that she could not remain
> hidden, she came trembling; and falling down before him,
> she declared in the presence of all the people why she had
> touched him, and how she had been immediately healed. He
> said to her, 'Daughter, your faith has made you well; go in
> peace.'
>
> —Luke 8:43–48 (NRSVA)

Praying responsively

In your holy presence,
we cannot remain hidden
The God who sees
Looks up and beholds us.

Collect for Midday

God at midday,
Would you who sustains us daily grant us what is needed to endure
until evening. As we return to our work, our relationships, all that

looms ahead, gift us with an imagination for life lived outside of the tyranny of exhaustion and dislocation. May the same magic that unites every part of you, so too keep us whole through our days—that we would know our bodies, that we would feel our emotions, and that we would remain near to our interior worlds, by the divine spirit which remembers us. *Amen.*

Silence may be kept

Psalm Reading

Can be replaced with a different psalm, song, or poem

Words in bold can be recited in unison by a collective

> When the LORD restored the fortunes of Zion,
> **we were like those who dream.**
> Then our mouth was filled with laughter
> **and our tongue with shouts of joy;**
> then it was said among the nations,
> 'The LORD has done great things for them.'
> **The LORD has done great things for us,**
> **and we rejoiced.**
>
> Restore our fortunes, O LORD,
> **like the watercourses in the Negeb.**
> May those who sow in tears
> **reap with shouts of joy.**
> Those who go out weeping,
> bearing the seed for sowing,
> **shall come home with shouts of joy,**
> **carrying their sheaves.**

> —Psalm 126: 1–6 (NRSVA)

Closing

May we endure the day, that we might meet rest in the night. Keep us in our bodies as we labor, as we dare to face the world again. And may our callings come to us with clarity, agency, and boundaries, that our dignity would be recognized not in our doing but in our very being, now and evermore. *Amen.*

Come, let us honor God with honest hearts.
And protect the earth and all she carries. *Amen.*

ALTERNATE PASSAGES BY CONCERN

Lament—Psalm 42:1–11; Jeremiah 9:17–24; John 11:1–35
Repair—Genesis 11:1–9; Zephaniah 3:9–20; Isaiah 55:1–13
Resistance—Exodus 1:8–20; Judges 4:4–22; Psalm 121
Liberation—Exodus 3:1–17; Isaiah 61:1–11; Psalm 146

3

DUSK

Wisdom

The guide begins

"If you listen closely in the night, you will hear your mother telling a story and at the end of the tale, she will ask you this question: 'Ou libéré?' Are you free, my daughter?" . . . "Now," she said, "you will know how to answer."

—Edwidge Danticat

Invitation

Words in bold can be recited in unison by a collective

It is in vain that you rise up early
and go late to rest,
eating the bread of anxious toil;
for [God] gives sleep to his beloved.

—Psalm 127:2 (NRSVA)

Yours is the day, **yours also the night;**
you established the luminaries and the sun.

—Psalm 74:16 (NRSVA)

Hymn

To be read or sung to music

LAY DIS BODY DOWN

Negro spiritual

I KNOW moon-rise, I know star-rise,
Lay dis body down;
I walk in de moonlight, I walk in de starlight,
To lay dis body down.
I walk in de graveyard, I walk troo de graveyard,
To lay dis body down.
I'll lie in de grass and stretch out my arms:
Lay dis body down.
I go to de judgment in de evenin' of de day,
When I lay dis body down;
And my soul and your soul will meet in de day
When I lay dis body down.

Psalm Reading

Can be replaced with a different psalm, song, or poem

Out of the depths I cry to you, LORD;
Lord, hear my voice.
Let your ears be attentive
to my cry for mercy.
If you, LORD, kept a record of sins,
Lord, who could stand?
But with you there is forgiveness,
so that we can, with reverence, serve you.
I wait for the LORD, my whole being waits,
and in his word I put my hope.
I wait for the Lord
more than watchmen wait for the morning,

more than watchmen wait for the morning.
Israel, put your hope in the LORD,
for with the LORD is unfailing love
and with him is full redemption.
He himself will redeem Israel
from all their sins.

—Psalm 130: 1–8 (NIV)

First Reading | *The Valley of Dry Bones*

Alternate passages from sacred literature may be read

The hand of the LORD came upon me, and he brought me out by
the spirit of the LORD and set me down in the middle of a valley;
it was full of bones. He led me all round them; there were very
many lying in the valley, and they were very dry. He said to me,
'Mortal, can these bones live?' I answered, 'O Lord GOD, you
know.' Then he said to me, 'Prophesy to these bones and say to
them: O dry bones, hear the word of the LORD. Thus says the
Lord GOD to these bones: I will cause breath to enter you, and
you shall live. I will lay sinews on you, and will cause flesh to
come upon you, and cover you with skin, and put breath in you,
and you shall live; and you shall know that I am the LORD.'

So I prophesied as I had been commanded; and as I prophesied, suddenly there was a noise, a rattling, and the bones came
together, bone to its bone. I looked, and there were sinews on
them, and flesh had come upon them, and skin had covered
them, but there was no breath in them; Then he said to me,
'Prophesy to the breath, prophesy, mortal, and say to the breath:
Thus says the Lord GOD: Come from the four winds, O breath,
and breathe upon these slain, that they may live.' I prophesied as
he commanded me, and the breath came into them, and they
lived and stood on their feet, a vast multitude.

Then he said to me, 'Mortal, these bones are the whole house
of Israel. They say, "Our bones are dried up, and our hope is lost;

we are cut off completely." Therefore prophesy, and say to them, Thus says the Lord GOD: I am going to open your graves, and bring you up from your graves, O my people; and I will bring you back to the land of Israel. And you shall know that I am the LORD, when I open your graves, and bring you up from your graves, O my people. I will put my spirit within you, and you shall live, and I will place you on your own soil; then you shall know that I, the LORD, have spoken and will act, says the LORD.'

—Ezekiel 37:1–14 (NRSVA)

Words in bold can be recited in unison by a collective

By day the LORD commands his steadfast love,
and at night his song is with me.

—Psalm 42:8 (NRSVA)

Second Reading | In the Flesh

Alternate passages from sacred literature may be read

The LORD is my shepherd; **I shall not want.**
He makes me lie down in green pastures;
he leads me beside still waters;
he restores my soul.
He leads me in right paths
for his name's sake.

Even though I walk through the darkest valley,
I fear no evil;
for you are with me;
your rod and your staff—
they comfort me.

You prepare a table before me
in the presence of my enemies;
you anoint my head with oil;
my cup overflows.

Surely goodness and mercy shall follow me
all the days of my life,
and I shall dwell in the house of the LORD
my whole life long.

—Psalm 23 (NRSVA)

Ancestors

It is so easy to be hopeful in the daytime when you can see
the things you wish on. But it was night, it stayed night.
Night was striding across nothingness with the whole round
world in his hands. . . . They sat in company with the others
in other shanties, their eyes straining against crude walls and
their souls asking if He meant to measure their puny might
against His. They seemed to be staring at the dark, but their
eyes were watching God.

—Zora Neale Hurston

The collective in unison

God Our Mother,
Forgive our unrest. Meet us now in tender mercy in our bodies, as
we hold space for every joy and every sorrow of the day.

Pause for brief silence

Steady us as we prepare to meet the dark. Cradle us in divine arms
and grant us courage to be held. As we prepare our souls for the
long night, may our breathing slow. May our muscles soften. Lay
us down in you. And guide us into rest, that we may dream. Glory
to the one who holds us and keeps us. *Amen.*

Praying responsively

The day is done, and the night unfurls before us.
Come, let us choose courage and silence.

Quiet our souls as we approach a sacred rest.
May we rise nearer to our souls than the day now past.

Collect for Dusk

God at dusk,
We remain. Through trial, through labor, through the terrors and beauties of this world, we're still here. Hearts drumming, lungs expanding. Help us remember that to simply go on is a triumph. As we recall our day, drive off the beast of anxiety that lurks in the corridors of our soul. Let us examine the day in truth, not as a ritual of self-hatred, but as a commitment to our own inner life and how our selfhood has engaged the exterior world. As evening falls, remind us that what we have given today is enough, that we might move toward rest without apology or guilt. As our eyes drift closed, remind us of the mysterious regeneration of our bodies, that we might marvel at our own renewal in the sacred dark. Make us dreamers this night, our imaginations liberated into a space without constraint. Let our rest be a portal to worlds known and unknown to us. And when we wake, we pray that the mystery of the night will have led us home to ourselves again. *Amen.*

Closing

As we are led into dreaming, may we find our bodies at rest against the chest of God, keeping rhythm with her breath. Together we hold the poet's words:

come celebrate
with me that everyday
something has tried to kill me
and has failed.

—Lucille Clifton

ALTERNATE PASSAGES BY CONCERN

Lament—Psalm 42:1–11; Jeremiah 9:17–24; John 11:1–35

Repair—Genesis 11:1–9; Zephaniah 3:9–20; Isaiah 55:1–13

Resistance—Exodus 1:8–20; Judges 4:4–22; Psalm 121

Liberation—Exodus 3:1–17; Isaiah 61:1–11; Psalm 146

4

ADVENT

To be prayed the four weeks leading to Christmas, or read during the Advent candle lighting each Sunday in Advent. The liturgy plays out in four movements: waiting, silence, embodiment, and darkness. All are conditions of the womb in a season when we remember the mystery of the divine born from Mary's body. Other familiar Advent movements are hope, joy, love, and peace; or death, judgment, heaven, and hell.

JOHN
by Lucille Clifton

somebody coming in blackness
like a star
and the world be a great bush
on his head
and his eyes be fire
in the city
and his mouth be true as time

he be calling the people brother
even in the prison
even in the jail

i'm just only a baptist preacher
somebody bigger than me coming
in blackness like a star

ADVENT I | WAITING

I would have despaired unless I had believed
that I would see the goodness of the LORD
In the land of the living.
Wait for the LORD;
Be strong and let your heart take courage;
Yes, wait for the LORD.

—Psalm 27:13–14 (NASB)

To be read in solitude or as a collective

God of the long wait,
We take hope, knowing you are a God whose movement is not
dependent on our ability to perceive it. Remind us that your wait
in the womb of Mary was not time wasted but an intimate beginning in mystery, growth, and dependency. Let our own waiting be
the same, that we would find ourselves able to trust our communities to sustain us, entering a safe and sacred interdependence for
all parts. As we wait for healing and liberation—in ourselves, in
the world—help us to practice justice, repair, and mercy, never
relying on the divine to absolve us of our collective and individual
responsibility. And let us wait in mystery, believing that those
who think they are in control of this world are not, and that oppression will not prevail. Help us to be at rest with the unknowing, that we would trust the secret of Mary's womb, realizing we
aren't entitled to knowledge or clarity, but are still held in love.
Let us feel that even here you are moving, you are growing our
way to life and healing. Protect us from despair as we wait for
liberation. *Amen.*

Breathe

INHALE: I grow weary of waiting.
EXHALE: God, keep me from despair.

Closing

Glory to the one who comes in flesh for all flesh. *Amen.*

ADVENT II | SILENCE

> Silence. Stillness. To give her soul a chance to attend its own affairs at its own level.
>
> —Toni Cade Bambara

To be read in solitude or as a collective

Silent God,

There are seasons when your silence feels like a cruel act of abandonment. We mistakenly equate nearness with noise. Show us a different kind of divine intimacy. A silence born not of neglect, but of safety and rest. In a world that weaponizes silence against the vulnerable, it is difficult to believe in its virtue. This Advent, allow us to ask the question of whose voice is being centered and whose is missing. Let those whose voices historically have taken up far too much space fall quiet in this season, in a silence of solidarity. Grant the marginalized the agency to choose their silences—not a forced silencing but a sacred rest and defiance in a world whose noise does not relent. If we're silent, let it be the quiet of Mary who kept her story close, allowing a small but sacred number to bear witness to her cosmic unfolding. If we're silent, let it be the silence of the womb, a warmth we can finally rest in. *Amen.*

Breathe

INHALE: The world grows loud.
EXHALE: I can rest in this silence.

INHALE: I can pause and listen.
EXHALE: Silence is a portal.

Closing

Glory to the one who comes in flesh for all flesh. *Amen.*

ADVENT III | EMBODIMENT

> I have the uncanny feeling that, just at the end of my life, I
> am beginning to reinhabit completely the body I long ago left.
>
> —Alice Walker

To be read in solitude or as a collective

God of the womb,

It is not lost on us that you submitted to the body of a woman, trusting in it to protect and grow you. As we remember the nine months you dwelt in the womb, the body of God being nurtured and carried, remind us that our own bodies are worthy of such care and tenderness. May this be a season of sacred pause, as we allow time to be near to our own bodies, to protect and strengthen them. In a world that demands so much of us, remind us that Christ did not come to us in physical independence, allowing the world to take and use him without limitation. Show us the face of the Christ who was gravely dependent, who needed to be held, fed, washed. Who needed to be soothed and rocked to sleep. If we are to honor the divine in us, may it be this divinity—fully embodied, fully dignified in the body. *Amen.*

Breathe

INHALE: The divine dwelled in a body.
EXHALE: This flesh is sacred.

Closing

Glory to the one who comes in flesh for all flesh. *Amen.*

ADVENT IV | DARKNESS

> Somebody told a lie one day. They couched it in language.
> They made everything black ugly and evil. Look in your
> dictionary and see the synonyms of the word *black*. It's
> always something degrading and low and sinister. Look at
> the word *white*, it's always something pure, high, and clean.
>
> —Martin Luther King, Jr.

> There is a reason the sky gets dark at night, we were not
> meant to see everything all the time. We were meant to rest
> and trust even in the darkness.
>
> —Morgan Harper Nichols

To be read in solitude or as a collective

God of the holy dark,
We know the truth. For too long we've been fed language that
communicates Black is dirty and bad, while white is pure and
safe. Reveal all the ways this is forming us; anti-Blackness seeping
into idiom and allegory, masquerading as poeticism. This Advent,
may we reclaim the sacred Black. As the days grow shorter and
the dark of night stretches, may we remember that Christ was
formed in the holy darkness of a womb—that our origin is not
the garden but the dark. May this be a season of deeper encounter
with the night. May the darkness guide us into deep rest, resisting
exhaustion and overexposure. May it be a darkness that opens us
to the unknown, that we would make peace with uncertainty and
marvel at mystery. And may it be a darkness that forms us into
people capable of holding the lament of others, that we would
never be too quick to turn on the light while someone else is
grieving. Hold us in the dark womb of Advent. Let us remember
what glory grows in the dark. *Amen.*

Breathe

INHALE: The world feels dim.
EXHALE: But glory grows in the dark.

Closing

Glory to the one who comes in flesh for all flesh. *Amen.*

5

CHRISTMASTIDE

Hope in a Cradle

Christmas night can feel like one of the saddest times of the year. For months, we have waited. As the days grew darker and colder, we wrote lists of all we wanted and tucked ornaments in trees. We counted down on felt calendars, our pockets filled with chocolates. For the four weeks of Advent, we named that we would not be rushed from our grief. We sang in anticipation, waiting for God to be born from a woman's womb. But now, after the thirty minutes it takes to open gifts, we can be left feeling aimless, deflated.

Christmas, it seems, is over precisely the hour it begins. It can never swell to joy because the celebration is snuffed out before we can even inhale. It hardly feels sincere that we are rushed from our joy as soon as the hope of the world is delivered into the world. The wait is long; we must feast with the same fervor as we fasted. We must celebrate with as much intention as we mourned.

In Christmastide, we give joy time to breathe. For twelve days, we bask in the reality that the divine cared enough about the oppressed that they were willing to abandon the privilege of paradise and be made mortal. Particularly the mortality of a babe—small and needy and powerless. Christ is not born self-sufficient but must rely on God's creation to be nurtured and sustained. How quickly do we rush God from womb to death? From manger to cross? Christmastide invites us into a slower story. A Christ who at present cannot speak, cannot teach—whose dignity, much like ours, is foremost in his very being. Behold, the child who drinks from Mary's breast. Listen as he stirs and cries through the night. This is a slow miracle. We pause. We behold.

To be read in solitude or as a collective

God with us,

We are in awe of you made child—small and needy and held. We are grateful to belong to a God who dares approach us with trust and tenderness. As we honor your birth, may the hope that has waned throughout the year be renewed; that we would know the world is more than death and decay. This Christmastide, may we rejoice in the beauty life contains. May we imagine the divine not just in the stories of your teaching and sacrifice, but also in the vulnerability of the divine child. Help us to weep. Remind us to never punish ourselves for asking for help, ridding us from the ways neediness has been demonized and mocked. Restore our trust, that just as a baby believes they will be carried, that they can cry and be fed, we would believe and find those whom we can trust. As we enter this season, help us to remember that hope is rarely ever sudden, but that it's okay if it grows on us slowly—as carefully as the hairs on our savior's head. God, make us small, that we would be held in you once again. *Amen.*

Breathe

INHALE: God was born.
EXHALE: I can rest in the beauty.

Closing

Glory to the one who comes in flesh for all flesh. *Amen.*

6

EPIPHANY

Epiphany is a day in Christian traditions when we remember the Magi's journey, following a star from nations around the world to meet Christ as an infant. Later, when King Herod attempts to manipulate them to reveal the location of the child he wants to kill, they, in sacred disobedience, ignore his request.

> And having been warned in a dream not to return to Herod, they left for their own country by another road.
>
> —Matthew 2:12 (NRSVA)

> Truth, by which the world is held together, has sprung from the earth, in order to be carried in a woman's arms.
>
> —Saint Augustine

To be read in solitude or as a collective

God of the Magi,
We hold close their demonstration of civil disobedience. When given the choice between the oppressive force of the empire and their responsibility to protect the life and dignity of the vulnerable, they listened to maker and not man. Would you preserve their story in us, that we might become faithful evaluators of the powers in our midst? Help us perceive all the ways the spirit of Herod is alive and well in our leaders—how they advocate for policies that benefit themselves and harm those they are meant to serve; how their words and requests, however subtle, have been poisoned by greed and power lust. Make ours a holy rebellion, held and led by those who have been discarded—a diverse number. We will listen as you guide us. Protect us as we make our way home. *Amen.*

Breathe

INHALE: They will not be gods to me.
EXHALE: I am free to walk away.

INHALE: God, guide my dreaming.
EXHALE: Show me the path to liberation.

Closing

Glory to the God who is known in the dark and in the light. *Amen.*

7

KWANZAA

To be read each morning of Kwanzaa or at the altar during the evening kinara lighting.

UMOJA | UNITY

Ancestors

> My humanity is bound up in yours, for we can only be human together.
>
> —Desmond Tutu

Wisdom

PAUL ROBESON
by Gwendolyn Brooks

That time
we all heard it,
cool and clear,
cutting across the hot grit of the day.
The major Voice.
The adult Voice
forgoing Rolling River,
forgoing tearful tale of bale and barge
and other symptoms of an old despond.
Warning, in music-words
devout and large,
that we are each other's

harvest:
we are each other's
business:
we are each other's
magnitude and bond.

Dreaming

God who gathers,
It is easy to forget we are mysteriously and intimately connected
in our Blackness—that liberation is not a solitary pursuit but the
responsibility of the collective. We confess that the oppressor has
indoctrinated us into the same narcissistic individualism that
plagues them. Protect us from this. Remind us that even our humanity does not exist in a vacuum, but flourishes with awareness
of how our existence is connected to the earth below our feet—
the waters that carry us, the fields that nourish us, the beauty
that reaches its hand out to us despite our neglect of it. Train us
toward a way of seeing the world that is grounded in umoja—in
sacred unity—that the weight of our hope might be shared, and
so, sustained. As we journey through Kwanzaa, may we grow
nearer to this mystery each day—by the memory of the altar, by
the light of the kinara, and by the words and song of the ancestors. *Ase.*

Breathe

INHALE: We breathe as one.
EXHALE: We get free together.

KUJICHAGULIA | SELF-DETERMINATION

Ancestors

The soul that is within me no man can degrade.

—Frederick Douglass

Dreaming

God who empowers,
We are tired of trying to survive under the thumb of whiteness.
Our oppressors make a show of "saving" us when in truth they are
the hand that demeans us. Thank you for making our dignity apparent in a world that doesn't always recognize it. Awaken that self-
determination which reminds us of our own agency. Make us wise
and discerning, that we would see opportunities for advancement
and ignore the voices that say we are unworthy. Let us move in a
sacred Black audacity. And in that belief, let us make our own
opportunities—our own paths to survival marked by the wisdom
and ways of our ancestors, the innovation and creativity of the
young. Grant us a self-determination that includes a fidelity to our
own bodies. That we would work and rest courageously, knowing
we have nothing to prove. *Ase.*

Breathe

INHALE: I am free to decide.
EXHALE: I want more for myself.

INHALE: I know my power.
EXHALE: My voice is sacred.

UJIMA | COLLECTIVE WORK AND RESPONSIBILITY

Ancestors

The changes we have to have in this country are going to be
for liberation of all people—because nobody's free until
everybody's free.

—Fannie Lou Hamer

Dreaming

God of the collective,
We are grateful that our divine maker does not desire us to be alone. Many of us long for connection and interdependence, but we have become used to enduring the sounds of our own loneliness. We confess that we've become so acquainted with loss and abandonment that we struggle to believe there are those who truly want to be with us. Keep us from pushing them away. Form us to be people of collective responsibility, that we would never become too familiar with solitary independence but would find ourselves participating in communal restoration and care. Let us find people who can hold our lament and rouse our laughter, those who can name their needs and allow space for ours. Let us belong to one another in true mutuality, knowing our burdens and hopes and liberation are mysteriously entwined. Let us bear it together. *Ase.*

Breathe

INHALE: I am not alone.
EXHALE: We will bear it together.

UJAMAA | COOPERATIVE ECONOMICS

Ancestors

So our people not only have to be reeducated to the importance of supporting black business, but the black man himself has to be made aware of the importance of going into business. And once you and I go into business, we own and operate at least the businesses in our community.

—Malcolm X

Dreaming

Abundant God,

Thank you for being a sustainer who cares deeply not just about provision but about inheritance. Restore what has been stolen from us and our ancestors. In the absence of the economic repair that is owed, we pray that you would invigorate Black businesses, organizations, and community efforts. We pray for a radical shift in the wealth distribution in this world, that those who have far too much would finally reckon with their own crooked reflections. That greed would be laid bare. That every thief will see their own hands clearly. And as we pray for provision and inheritance, keep us from that guilt which uses scripture and false virtue to shame us for wanting economic advancement. Rend every lie that tells us that we were meant for scarcity when we know you are a God of abundance. Help us to ask boldly, that we would have enough to build up our communities and sustain the life that you have graciously given to us. *Ase.*

Breathe

INHALE: You are not a God of scarcity.
EXHALE: Let us walk in abundance.

INHALE: There's enough for us.
EXHALE: We claim it.

NIA | PURPOSE

Ancestors

You have to go the way your blood beats. If you don't live the only life you have, you won't live some other life, you won't live any life at all.

—James Baldwin

Dreaming

God who calls,
May we listen. We are grateful that the divine stirs in us a momentum toward particular giftings and desires. Help us to listen for what's true in us, that we would enter our purpose freely. Keep us from being enticed by missions and goals that are grounded outside of our deepest values. Liberate us from that sinister temptation to build our lives on the quicksand of toxic individualism. Make our calling both personal and collective, that our hopes would be grafted onto the shared hope that has sustained our people across time. *Ase.*

Breathe

INHALE: I know who I am.
EXHALE: I will walk in it.

INHALE: God, keep me in my purpose
EXHALE: that my community would flourish.

KUUMBA | CREATIVITY

Ancestors

The precise role of the artist, then, is to illuminate that darkness, blaze roads through that vast forest, so that we will not, in all our doing, lose sight of its purpose, which is, after all, to make the world a more human dwelling place.

—James Baldwin

Art invites us to know beauty and to solicit it from even the most tragic of circumstances. Art reminds us that we belong here. And if we serve, we last.

—Toni Morrison

Dreaming

Creative God,

Thank you for creating. Thank you for showing us the honor and gift of being able to make something out of our deepest sorrows and joys. We pray that you would protect our capacity for dreaming and creating, that those who seek to diminish our art would be confounded by our unending creativity. In profound mystery, help us to harness beauty from a world that doesn't always acknowledge ours. Grant us defiant imaginations for what could be that isn't yet, knowing we will survive by our dreaming. Let our poems break chains. Let our songs coil through the brains of our children. Let our paintings jolt the dead to life. Cradle every creative whim, God, that we would craft something not for the consumption and regurgitation of the world but for the welfare of those who honor us. *Ase.*

Breathe

INHALE: In beauty, I am made.
EXHALE: And beauty I will make.

IMANI | FAITH

Wisdom

"You say, 'Our bones are dried up, and our hope is lost; we are cut off.' But O my people, behold: I will open and raise you from your graves. I will attach tendons to you and swaddle you in flesh and skin. And I will bring you into the land that was promised to you—your own land. O dry bones, I can and will breathe you back to life."

—Paraphrased from Ezekiel 37:11–14

Ancestors

I believe in living.
I believe in birth.
I believe in the sweat of love
and in the fire of truth.
And i believe that a lost ship,
    steered by tired, seasick sailors,
can still be guided home
to port.

—Assata Shakur

Dreaming

Our Sacred Hope,
It is calming to be at rest among those who love us. Let us pause to feel the warmth of this kinara, to behold the faces on the altar, knowing that we have dreamt up and reclaimed a spirituality for our own sake. Remind us that we gather as people of profound faith—not a faith that is captive to any one religion, but faith in the memory and imagination and force of Black souls in the world. Faith that our struggle will not always be so. As we cultivate new rituals and expand our imagination for communing with the divine, may we never be suffocated by the expectations of others. Grant us courage to truly expand, even within this room; that we would be free to hold the sacred in whichever hand feels right to us today. *Ase.*

Breathe

INHALE: I belong to the story of freedom.
EXHALE: I was born from the womb of hope.

8

ASH WEDNESDAY

"For dust you are
and to dust you will return."

—Genesis 3:19 (NIV)

But still, like dust, I'll rise.

—Maya Angelou

Mortal Hope

"Ashes to ashes, dust to dust." When God spoke these words in the garden, did their voice crack? Did their hands tremble as they then knelt to make clothes that would cover the glory they birthed? These words came to us as shame entered the world—and out of shame, all manner of suffering. They were not a proclamation of punishment but a reminder of Eve and Adam's finitude. It's a poem of grief and memory. *Ashes to ashes, dust to dust.* There is beauty in our humanity. Peer down in the cool, dark ash; there is death there. Watch the particles lift and sway in the wind; there is yet life. . . .

On Ash Wednesday we are marked on our foreheads with a re- minder of our mortality. The same palms we raise up and wave on Palm Sunday each year are made to know the sting of death—we burn them. And the following year, in an ever-curious act, we pick up the ashes and we mark ourselves with them.

What does it mean that we don't just talk about the ashes, or even reverently observe them, but that we physically smear them across our faces? Perhaps, in the marking, we approach solidarity. We re- member that the same fate that haunts you, haunts me. The same beauty that birthed you, lives in me. And that this comes as a mark on the body, I think, reminds us that the Lenten journey of self-examination is deeply entwined with the physical world.

As we mark ourselves with these ashes, we remind ourselves that no grief is solitary. That what has stricken you is also carried by me. We begin our Lenten journey together, reminding one another that we are those whose flesh grows back. We are those who remain. It is not easy, but we cling to this: God has always seen sacred potential in the dust.

To be read in solitude or as a collective

God of the Ashes,

Today, let us hold the tension of the story of our making—born of the dirt, beautifully connected to the earth we walk on. And yet, possessing the knowledge of our own mortality—that our common decay cannot be escaped. As we begin Lent, help us to become honest about the ways our societies and selfhoods are marred by injustice, cruelty, neglect, and greed. Help us to see our own role in the degeneration of the world; that as we push back evil around us, we might also admit those secret evils that dwell in us. As we name how we've been complicit in the ashes of this world, help us to bear them in solidarity and hope. *Amen.*

Breathe

INHALE: I will carry the ashes.
EXHALE: God, bring rest to the suffering.

INHALE: There is breath in these ashes.
EXHALE: No death is final.

9

LENT

"Is not this the kind of fasting I have chosen:
to loose the chains of injustice
and untie the cords of the yoke,
to set the oppressed free
and break every yoke?
Is it not to share your food with the hungry
and to provide the poor wanderer with shelter—
when you see the naked, to clothe them,
and not to turn away from your own flesh and blood?
Then your light will break forth like the dawn,
and your healing will quickly appear;
then your righteousness will go before you,
and the glory of the LORD will be your rear guard.
Then you will call, and the LORD will answer;
you will cry for help, and he will say: Here am I.

"If you do away with the yoke of oppression,
with the pointing finger and malicious talk,
and if you spend yourselves in behalf of the hungry
and satisfy the needs of the oppressed,
then your light will rise in the darkness,
and your night will become like the noonday.
The LORD will guide you always;
he will satisfy your needs in a sun-scorched land."

—Isaiah 58:6–11 (NIV)

Lent is a wilderness carved out in space and time with prayer. . . . There *is* more than one kind of wilderness. There is the wilderness of the soul, an often lonely, aching place.

There is the wilderness of the world, a place where words of love are everywhere yet people hunger for love because the imitations of love that perfuse our society leave us empty, aching, hungry.

—Dr. Wilda C. Gafney

Heard in the Wilderness

Could you wander for forty years if it meant freedom? If you listen, you can still hear them groaning—they who were rescued, only to find that freedom is never so easily won. That liberation is a path marked by uncertainty and thirst and grief over all that was lost in the revolution. In Exodus, we are faced with a God of slow rescue. When the struggle of the wilderness became apparent, even the Israelites themselves began to pine for the bondage of Pharaoh. How fierce the grip of certainty—to know with clarity what is to come, however terrible and lonesome that fate might be.

Perhaps God knew that part of liberation is confronting anything you might hunger for more than it. Will you cry out longing for the chains that once held you? The wilderness is uncharted, and humans are prone to willful amnesia. We'd rather forget and return to bondage than remember and wade in the unknown. We grow numb.

Assata Shakur wrote, "People get used to anything. The less you think about your oppression, the more your tolerance for it grows. . . . But to become free, you have to be acutely aware of being a slave." And the freer one gets, the more their hunger for liberation loudens. All the false appetites that spoke over this chief desire begin to quiet.

How does your hunger sound? What are the whispers of desire that drive you?

For forty days leading to the remembrance of the death of Christ, we commit to remembering our chains. We make our home in the wilderness—in the liminal spaces where liberation has begun but sorrow and hunger remain. In this season, we choose solidarity with all who are suffering—the displaced, the abused, the oppressed and neglected.

Many of us have been trained to believe Lent is about solidarity with Christ alone. But Christ's forty days in the desert mirror the forty years the Israelites journeyed in the wilderness after being rescued from slavery. The two journeys remind us that the wilderness can be both solitary and communal. That it can defy both the systems and powers of the exterior world, and the despair of one's interior world. And that these were two physical desert journeys speaks to a necessarily embodied liberation.

As we move in solidarity, we remind ourselves presence is not solidarity. Knowledge is not solidarity. Solidarity is the kind of unity that costs us something. And we choose a form for our fasting that is not about the self, but about those who are most vulnerable. And for those who are suffering and in need, we must grab hold of a charity to self and take a posture of receiving. Lent shifts the scales of the cosmos back toward a balance of provision and justice. In Lent, there are those of us who will position our souls toward sacrifice, and some who will rightfully receive what has been kept from them. Every role holy and necessary for the healing of all.

So, despite prevalent teachings, the question of this sacred season is not, *What food are you giving up for Lent?* It is, *What practice of solidarity with the suffering are you choosing?* Or, *What needs do you need met this Lent?* We honor the complexity of hunger and desire, and we find ourselves liberated into a season not rooted in scarcity, but in justice, healing, and the welfare of those who have long awaited their portion.

To be prayed individually or as a collective weekly during Lent

LENT I | HUNGER

I would hurl words into this darkness and wait for an echo, and if an echo sounded, no matter how faintly, I would send other words to tell, to march, to fight, to create a sense of the hunger for life that gnaws in us all.

—Richard Wright

God of deep hunger,
We thank you for being a God who is unconcerned with spiritual practices that don't affirm the dignity of the most vulnerable. Keep us from shallow spiritualities that are more concerned with obedience to ritual than how that ritual should bring about justice and restoration in the world. Retrain our appetites toward healing and liberation. If we fast this Lent, let it be in that ancient way, which gives our portions to the hungry and oppressed. And if we have need, let this be a season of reclamation, that we would accept what is owed to us, that we would take all that our dignity demands. Grant that we would find our own healing magnified as we participate in the healing of the cosmos. And let our darkest nights amplify the light, that we would look up and see no less than the very face of God in one another. *Amen.*

Breathe

INHALE: Lord, transform my hungers.
EXHALE: Let my desire be for justice.

LENT II | MORTALITY

In becoming forcibly and essentially aware of my mortality, and of what I wished and wanted for my life, however short it might be, priorities and omissions became strongly etched in a merciless light, and what I most regretted were my silences. Of what had I ever been afraid?

—Audre Lorde

God who died,
We are heavy with grief. We've been promised freedom in the divine, but this wilderness reeks of death. The landscape is so thorny

that we're beginning to feel nothing at all. We feel betrayed and confused and tired, God. Please, not one more thing. Just let us live. Let us heal. This Lent, instill among us rituals of remembrance that allow space for rest and wailing. Relieve any pressure we feel to resolve our pain before we've truly felt it. And as we're healing, grant us a wisdom to know we don't have to carry every sadness all at once. Walk with us as we protect our minds and bodies from despair. *Amen.*

Breathe

INHALE: We honor our mortality.
EXHALE: Hope is written in the ashes.

INHALE: What rest was stolen from us in life,
EXHALE: may we meet in death.

LENT III | GRIEF

Gloom crawls around
lapping lasciviously
between my toes, at my ankles,
and it sucks the strands of my
hair. It forgives my heady
fling with Hope. I am
joined again into its
greedy arms.

—Maya Angelou

God who knows loss,
We long for the presence of those we've lost—the sound of their voice, their laughter, the way their face moved. A longing so deep, it is difficult to articulate. Keep it from consuming us. Protect our grief from the grip of despair, and guide us into the kind of re-

membrance that leads to healing and a clarity of self. Keep watch, too, over those of us who endure the complexity of losing the imperfect—those who both loved us and have hurt us. Keep us from that cheap form of remembrance that reduces those we've loved into faultless, polished, uncomplicated caricatures. Let us recall them in the fullness of their humanity. And as we behold their passing into your arms, into the arms of the ancestors, may some portion of their peace find its way to us. *Amen.*

Breathe

INHALE: I can grieve in the wilderness.
EXHALE: I will not look away from suffering.

INHALE: I don't have to pretend.
EXHALE: I can honor my pain.

LENT IV | TRUTH-TELLING

People who shut their eyes to reality simply invite their own destruction, and anyone who insists on remaining in a state of innocence long after that innocence is dead turns himself into a monster.

—James Baldwin

Honest God,

We confess that we, as individuals and nations, have engaged in self-protection and delusion. Let this be a season when we reclaim the practice of telling the truth about our histories, that we would no longer shield ourselves and others from the harm we have caused by coddling our guilt and insecurity. Let our love be made of unapologetic truth-telling. Let those of us who have been gaslit find our stories centered and affirmed in this season. Guide us toward spaces that have grown weary of delusions, desiring to see the world for what it is, in all its complexities, beauties, tragedies, and oppression. And as we cultivate honest communities, let our healing and liberation rise to meet us. *Amen.*

Breathe

INHALE: I am not who I was.
EXHALE: I forgive myself.

LENT V | SOLIDARITY

I am often struck by the dangerous narcissism fostered by spiritual rhetoric that pays so much attention to individual self-improvement and so little to the practice of love within the context of community.

—bell hooks

God of Solidarity,
Thank you for being a God who enters the suffering of the world—who doesn't run from those in pain but rushes to the site of blood, of tears. Release us from empty cravings of unity that come at no cost to the oppressor, and guide us toward a solidarity that demands something of us. Let us learn to risk ourselves on behalf of the vulnerable, believing that when one of us is harmed, we all are. Help us to remember that justice and liberation are not a scarcity, and that our survival and dignity are wrapped up in one another. And God, keep us from those who will demonize the fight in us. Who would prefer us complacent and far from one another. Secure in us the courage to stand, knowing together we will restore what the world has tried to suffocate in us. *Amen.*

Breathe

INHALE: I journey to the margins.

EXHALE: I protect every corner.

INHALE: I know the cost.

EXHALE: I choose solidarity.

Benediction

Praise to the God who is well acquainted with the wilderness but will never abandon us to it. *Amen.*

1 0

PALM SUNDAY

Jesus found a young donkey and sat on it; As it is written:
'Do not be afraid, daughter of Zion.
Look, your king is coming,
sitting on a donkey's colt!'

—John 12:14–15 (NRSVA)

There is miracle in belonging to a God who rejects the image of a gloried hero and instead comes to us on a donkey, centering the plight of those who suffer.

Liberation begins with this: Do not be afraid.

God of the Palms,
Thank you for drawing near to us. We have known what it is to encounter "help" that isn't truly help. We have known white savior complexes and the narrative of white heroism, which has always secretly delighted in suffering, so it might be the hero again and again. Thank you for showing us a different way: a God who rejects privilege, a God who is unbothered by sitting on a donkey if it means you are drawing near to us. As we wait, take away the fear that has settled on our souls. Help us to trust in the arrival of goodness even in the wake of suffering. Let this Palm Sunday speak the language of welcome; that we would never turn hope away when it appears to us. *Amen.*

Breathe

INHALE: Do not be afraid.
EXHALE: Liberation is coming.

MAUNDY THURSDAY

Then he poured water into a basin and began to wash the
disciples' feet and to wipe them with the towel that was tied
around him. He came to Simon Peter, who said to him, 'Lord,
are you going to wash my feet?' Jesus answered, 'You do not
know now what I am doing, but later you will understand.'

—John 13:5–7 (NRSVA)

Christ's death begins with a meal. "Eat, drink." That we would
remember him in our bodies. Then, God kneels in his body to
wash the bodies in his company. This is more than mere
symbolism. The path to liberation is to stay in our bodies.

Embodied God,
At the door of trauma, you remind us that it is glory to be in our own
flesh. We thank you that when you asked us to remember you, you
asked us to eat, to drink—that we would meet something of you in the
act of nourishment. Guide us back to an embodied existence, and help
us to be patient and gentle with those times when we feel we must
leave our bodies to survive. God, we ache. The traumas and tragedies
of this world land heavily on our physical selves. Would you grant us a
liberation that is not simply a project of the mind or the spirit, but that
has implications for our daily physical conditions. That as we attune to
our bodies, our shoulders could relax, our jaws slacken, our breath become deep. As we move toward justice and solidarity, may we befriend
the gloried physical in all tenderness and compassion. *May it be so.*

Breathe

INHALE: Suffering surrounds me.
EXHALE: God, help me stay in my body.

1 2

GOOD FRIDAY

By oppression and judgment he was taken away.
Yet who of his generation protested?
For he was cut off from the land of the living;
for the transgression of my people he was punished.
He was assigned a grave with the wicked,
and with the rich in his death,
though he had done no violence,
nor was any deceit in his mouth.

—Isaiah 53:8–9 (NIV)

Until we can see the cross and the lynching tree together,
until we can identify Christ with a "recrucified" black body
hanging from a lynching tree, there can be no genuine
understanding of Christian identity in America, and no
deliverance from the brutal legacy of slavery and white
supremacy.

—James H. Cone

The cross can heal and hurt; it can be empowering and
liberating but also enslaving and oppressive. . . . I believe that
the cross placed alongside the lynching tree can help us to
see Jesus in America in a new light, and thereby empower
people who claim to follow him to take a stand against white
supremacy and every kind of injustice.

—James H. Cone

God of the long night,
Thank you for being a God not just of solidarity but of deep and
raw emotion. A God who did not endure violence in silence but who

spoke and cried as your body was broken on the cross. Help us to understand that our memory of you becomes more whole when we remember you alongside the injustices with which you suffered in solidarity: the hunger, the abuse, the loneliness of the world. Today let us grieve the path of the cross—illness, violence, alienation, the degradation of land, and all pain unspoken. Let us weep and rest. Reveal yourself to us, remind us of a God who knows the weight of oppression, and help us believe that truly you are with us. That your cause is our cause—no less than justice and liberation in life and death. *Amen.*

Breathe

INHALE: This is too much to hold.
EXHALE: I can grieve with God.

SILENT SATURDAY

'For there is hope for a tree, if it is cut down, that it will sprout again, and that its shoots will not cease.'

—Job 14:7 (NRSVA)

Holy Saturday may be the most liminal space in the Christian liturgical cycle. Passion has become pathos. The death of Jesus stupefies, but the breaking dawn has not dispelled the waking dream. Yet the liturgical remembrance is part of a thousands-year-old cycle, and we know what the next dawn brings. We struggle not to anticipate that dawn. These lessons underscore our finitude, our mortality and that of all living things, and the mortality of Jesus, Son of Woman, Son of God, Child of Earth.

—Dr. Wilda C. Gafney

The waiting of Silent Saturday is the triumph of injustice, alienation, and violence—all without a word from God. You don't have to pretend the wait isn't agony. If it feels like God is silent, say so. Your doubts, your grief, are safe here.

Silent Saturday trains us in the liminal, as we make space for a pain that doesn't immediately resolve. How does the silence of God form us? What do you hear in the silence? Sometimes our grief is the most sacred sound.

Even the silence
has a story to tell you.
Just listen. Listen.

—Jacqueline Woodson

God of the liminal,
When we take account of the tragedies of the world, it is difficult to believe there is a powerful and loving God. Are you really with us? Why won't you intervene to bring justice and healing now? We trust that you are patient with these doubts. A God who is not threatened by our unbelief but draws near to us in it. Help us toward an understanding of you that includes tension and mystery. Let us be empathetic with our souls, which have endured so much suffering and have a right to ask deep questions of our maker. But as we do, let us find an empathy for you—a God who is no stranger to suffering but endures all things with us, that we might find full liberation. Let our doubts lead us into deeper intimacy with the divine, as we tell the truth of the questions that plague us. *Amen.*

Breathe

INHALE: God, why are you silent?
EXHALE: I'll hold hope as I wait.

INHALE: I won't be rushed from grieving.
EXHALE: I can rest in this silence.

EASTER

Of course he wasn't dead. He could never be dead until she
herself had finished feeling and thinking. The kiss of his
memory made pictures of love and light against the wall.
Here was peace. She pulled in her horizon like a great fish-
net. Pulled it from around the waist of the world and draped
it over her shoulder. So much of life in its meshes! She called
in her soul to come and see.

—Zora Neale Hurston

It mattered not how long he had wandered in the wilderness,
how long they had kept him in chains, how long he had
helped them and kept himself in his own chains; none of
that mattered now. . . . It mattered only that those kind of
chains were gone and that he had crawled out into the
clearing and was able to stand up on his hind legs and look
around and appreciate the difference between then and now,
even on the awful Richmond days when the now came
dressed as the then.

—Edward P. Jones

Easter holds memory for a God who came back to life still bearing
scars. We're reminded that we don't have to leave behind our grief
to participate in the joy of liberation. Our scars remain, but we
don't need to dismiss our grief to participate in the joy of
liberation.

On this mountain, God will prepare
a feast for all people.
On this mountain, God will destroy
the veil that covers all nations.

God will swallow up death forever,
and wipe away the tears from every face,
and shame will be cast out from all the earth.

—Paraphrased from Isaiah 25:6–8

God who rose,

Resurrect us. We've belonged to communities, workplaces, and spiritual spaces that have demanded our death far more than they ever advocated for our life. They ask us to "die to self," the ambiguity of the command like grabbing a knife by its blade. No longer will we mirror the hands of neglect that the world uses daily. Let joy find us today. Remind us that any spirituality which is always death, never resurrection, is a farce. What liberation we taste today, may we crave in full as we refuse to wander back to the chains that once held us. May joy find us. Not a joy absent of story or sorrow, but a joy whose allegiance is to memory. A joy that is not quick to forget the agony of Good Friday or dismiss the doubt of Silent Saturday. May we remember and rise to meet hope nonetheless, knowing our liberation is whispering up at us from its empty grave. *Amen.*

Breathe

INHALE: God is alive.
EXHALE: And God's breath is freedom.

INHALE: Liberation comes in a body.
EXHALE: I will honor mine.

PENTECOST

And how is it that we hear, each of us, in our own native language?

—Acts 2:8 (NRSVA)

We die. That may be the meaning of life. But we do language. That may be the measure of our lives.

—Toni Morrison

The Sound of Wholeness

It began with a strong wind. Then something like tongues of fire began to divide and rest on each person gathered. I can't tell you if they were afraid, if their eyes widened and hearts raced. If they thought to hide, be it from the fire or from one another. But I can tell you that in mystery and all at once, people in the room began to utter tongues unknown to them. An utterance that went out to the multitude, people from every nation, as the sacred sound drew them toward one another. They heard *themselves* in the sound—not the language of their oppressors or people who believed themselves to be closer to the divine than others. They each heard their own language and understood. What words were spoken remain as mysterious as the tongues that bore them. But together, even in the presence of doubt, people from all nations remembered their ancestors. Those who had an imagination for a miracle such as this. The image of God, a sacred multitude, gathered in the midst of a cosmic power shift.

In her 1993 Nobel Lecture, Toni Morrison tells a parable of language and its capacity to destroy or liberate depending on how we wield it.

The conventional wisdom of the Tower of Babel story is that the collapse was a misfortune. That it was the distraction, or the weight of many languages that precipitated the tower's failed architecture. That one monolithic language would have expedited the building and heaven would have been reached. Whose heaven, she wonders? And what kind? Perhaps the achievement of Paradise was premature, a little hasty if no one could take the time to understand other languages, other views, other narratives period. Had they, the heaven they imagined might have been found at their feet.

Could it be that Pentecost is paradise remembered on earth? What does it mean that in the story we are not told precisely *what* they communicated about the miracle or the divine? We know only that it was understood—that no tribe or tongue was excluded nor made a singular spectacle, but that a collective was born.

Two thousand years after the Tower of Babel falls and fifty days after Christ rises from the dead, we find the story of Pentecost. The Spirit descends upon a sacred diverse gathering, and language is made portal to the divine. A path to God, to one another, and to shared imagination. Pentecost reminds us that the Spirit of God rejects assimilation under the guise of "unity." This tale is not just about diversity; it's not mere tokenism; it's language as liberation. It's the sound of excluded voices making something whole again.

For the multitude

God of every tongue,
We are grateful that in the presence of the Spirit, we are not asked to forget ourselves but to remember. To remember where we came from, to recall the sound of our own cultures and languages. Help us to heal from those spaces that have demanded assimilation from us under the guise of unity. To belong, we are told we must exalt commonality over particularity. Teach us the kind of belonging that it is not threatened by those things that make us different but

comes alive at the site of inclusion. Protect us from communities who only welcome our cultures as a theatrical symbol of their own benevolence. Lead us into spaces where our presence is longed for not as a mark of achievement but out of the deep recognition that hope cannot survive on one tongue alone. *Amen.*

Breathe

INHALE: I won't forget myself.
EXHALE: I will listen for my voice.

16

MOTHER'S DAY

Out of the corner of one eye, I could see my mother. Out of the corner of the other eye, I could see her shadow on the wall, cast there by the lamp-light. It was a big and solid shadow, and it looked so much like my mother that I became frightened. For I could not be sure whether for the rest of my life I would be able to tell when it was really my mother and when it was really her shadow standing between me and the rest of the world.

—Jamaica Kincaid

Perhaps I can say this all more simply; I say the love of women healed me.

—Audre Lorde

God Our Mother,

We thank you for grounding your character in the tenderness, protection, and even sorrow of a mother. To know that no human experience—mother or child—is far from you gives us permission to uncover the particularities of how we were made to love and be loved. On this day, we're reminded that we do not begin with ourselves. Our beauty, our pain, do not exist in a vacuum but are tethered to those who've come before us. We pray for the mothers who have protected us, who are weary, who have stayed, who have left, who are grieving, who are proud—understanding that the story of what it means to be a mother is not singular. And as children, would you remind us that it is okay to lament the ways we have not been loved well, while also celebrating the miracle and mystery of those who loved us fiercely. We are made of more than us. Help us to behold it. *Amen.*

FATHER'S DAY

"There you saw how the LORD your God carried you, as a
father carries his son, all the way you went until you reached
this place."

—Deuteronomy 1:31 (NIV)

You are growing into consciousness, and my wish for you is
that you feel no need to constrict yourself to make other
people comfortable.

—Ta-Nehisi Coates

God of tenderness,
We thank you for our fathers. Those with us and those gone before
us. Those who held us and showed us what it means to belong to one
another. In a society that often demands a singular portrait of the
masculine, awaken memories and stories of the tenderness of fa-
therhood, that our narrative would not allow the men in our lives to
be reduced. Grant those who have longed for their father more than
they have been held by him the space to lament, to grieve in the
way that they need to. Place people in their lives to remind them
they are no less worthy of love. Liberate them to name their deepest longings, that they would not be rushed from their grieving.
May they be held and loved and known. *Amen.*

1 8

JUNETEENTH

Ancestors

Freeing yourself was one thing, claiming ownership of that
freed self was another.

—Toni Morrison

Dreaming

Words in bold can be recited in unison by a collective

God of broken chains,
On this day, we remember. We do not know how it felt when the
word of freedom came—what release was felt in the bodies of
those who made us, what disbelief, what joy, what sorrow. But
would you allow some echo of it to resound in our bodies today?
We gather not just to honor freedom rung, but in protection and
continuation of it. Let it resound clearly as we join voices on
this day:

We pray peace and deep rest for our ancestors. Those who labored
without agency over their bodies for generations, and those who
chose the sea.
Holding memory, we proclaim:
We will not be owned.

We marvel at the dreamers—those who clung to an imagination
for liberation regained. Those who fought, strategized, organized.
Holding memory, we proclaim:
We will not be owned.

We thank you for those who became our own historians—who preserved culture in whispers by moonlight, transmitting song and name.
Holding memory, we proclaim:
We will not be owned.

We grieve for the brutality of families alienated from one another, the daughter ripped from her mother's breast, sister torn from brother. And we honor all the ways our people formed new familial bonds, rising to nurture children and impart tenderness on those the oppressor sought to harden. Strengthen our own bonds now, that the invisible thread stretching between each holy Black soul would be fortified by compassion and intergenerational healing.
Holding memory, we proclaim:
We will not be owned.

God, we pause for every body broken, bruised, and lynched. There are stories that reside in our bodies both known and unknown to us. Keep us near to our own flesh, that we would protect one another from the brutality of white capitalism. May the rest and care that were denied to our ancestors be found in us today.
Holding memory, we proclaim:
We will not be owned.

And this joy in us, this durable, defiant joy, would you shield it from the mouth of despair? Remind us there is no void that can match the strength of our collective hope. Keep our songs alive, every verse, every dance. May our humor survive, as we play and laugh. Show us the many faces of joy, that all who dare encounter it will find themselves at home.
Holding memory, we proclaim:
We will not be owned.

Now may the same God who spoke to Harriet make the sound of liberation clear as night to us. May the divine hold us in the same holy darkness that protected our ancestors on the journey. And as we remember, may they shield us from despair, knowing that our story is more than pain. Ours is the story of dignity. Let us reclaim it. *Ase.*

Breathe

INHALE: Liberation is ours.

EXHALE: God, teach me the sound of freedom.

BIRTH

Observing any human being from infancy, seeing someone
come into existence . . . must be something wonderful to
behold; to see experience collect in the eyes, around the
corners of the mouth, the weighing down of the brow, the
heaviness in heart and soul, the thick gathering around the
waist, the breasts, the slowing down of footsteps not from old
age but only with the caution of life . . . the pleasure for the
observer, the beholder, is an invisible current between the
two, observed and observer, beheld and beholder, and I
believe that no life is complete, no life is really whole,
without this invisible current, which is in many ways a
definition of love.

—Jamaica Kincaid

ENTRANCE

A Black
baby girl
was born yesterday.
Who will tell her
it's not true
what they say about her?
Come, let us
swaddle her in truth:
It sounds like,
no one can give you freedom
because your blood cannot be chained.
It sounds like,
    be gentle with yourself, we buried miracle in your bones.

God of first breaths,

This is miracle. We've waited. We've witnessed as they grew and floated and stretched in the womb. The child we welcome is one of the deepest mysteries we've known. We are prepared and unprepared; ready to love as best we can but riddled with self-doubt. We are eager and tired; knowing we must find some way to care for ourselves, to rest and attend to our bodies, as we learn to care for the body of another. And still, God, we are afraid. This world is home to measureless beauty and incessant terrors. As we look into this child's face, we want all of the joy and none of the pain that awaits them. May we serve as a harbor for them, that they would be safe with us, never dismissed and always respected. Keep us from the kind of fear that will tempt us to control this child more than love them. And that which they cannot be protected from, may you grant them the resources, community, and stability of heart to heal from. Release us from any delusion that this child is ours to own, that they exist to fulfill our own hopes for them. Remind us that they are not a salve for our loneliness or own needs, but a full human with their own distinct path. For as long as they journey with us, may they always remain near to their own souls, grounded in a sense of self that includes us but is not defined by us.

As we cradle this child, may any good that runs through us flow into them. May we teach them. May we watch over them. May we believe them. And may the dignity inherent to them be revealed to them daily. Glory to God for the mystery of every born thing. *Amen.*

20

REUNION

Ancestors

May we never forget the beauty of what we saw and did—
and the untranslatable experience of being loved deeply and
blackly.

—Robin Coste Lewis

Raising Black children—female and male—in the mouth of
a racist, sexist, suicidal dragon is perilous and chancy. If they
cannot love and resist at the same time, they will probably
not survive.

—Audre Lorde

Dreaming

Words in bold can be recited in unison by a collective

God of the long table,
We are made of gratitude today. That we can gather across generations and households is a rare gift not lost on us. We thank you for
every face before us and those who could not be with us. Use this
time to knit us together, weaving disparate parts back toward a
shared origin. Help us to see the beauty in this belonging.

Let us laugh—teeth bared, bellies taut, resurrecting inside jokes
and spinning monologues. May our laughter flow through our
bodies freely and unsuppressed.
With one voice we pray:
We're still here.

Let us eat—every plate, flowing with memory and the wonder of
our gramma's kitchen, recipes preserved like sacred artifacts. May
our seconds be as blessed as our firsts.
With one voice we pray:
We're still here.

Let us remember—all that has made us and is still making us.
May stories flow out of us and be met with grave attention, that
one day the stories can be passed on and inherited by our young.
With one voice we pray:
We're still here.

Yes, we pray for our young—bring our gazes down to meet them
eye to eye. May we listen to them and take them seriously,
welcoming them fully into the fold even now. God, have mercy
and protect them in all the ways we are unable to.
With one voice we pray:
We're still here.

And we pray for any who do not feel at rest in this space. Be near
to them as they connect in the way that feels safe and good to
them.
With one voice we pray:
We're still here.

Restore those bonds that have been made frail by time and
distance. Help us to remember that no two relationships are alike,
as we release any expectations we place on others for deeper
intimacy than what feels true. Let us be patient with our love as
we return to one another.
With one voice we pray:
We're still here.

And let joy ring out from us. In memory of all we and our ancestors have endured—even still, we remain. We're still here, breathing freely. Remaining not despite our story but because of it. And for this we celebrate. We exhale. This is sacred air. This is holy ground. *Amen.*

HOMEGOING

Ancestors

My heart cannot confront
this death without relief
My soul will not control
this leaking of my grief

And this is for Crazy Horse singing as he dies
And here is my song of the living
who must sing against the dying
sing to join the living
with the dead

—June Jordan

Dreaming

Words in bold can be recited in unison by a collective

God who knows death,
We come before you with an ache we can't articulate. A void has appeared in our midst. This passing has altered so much of what we know and remember—Christmas mornings and birthday parties, goodnight stories and school pickups, car rides and kitchen talks. As we grieve the departure of one we loved, help us to feel what we feel, be it sadness or anger or nothing at all. Remind us that grief has many faces and no timeline. Grant us both patience and honesty. Keep us from idealizing or demonizing them in death, but protect our memory that we would recall them for who they truly were to us, and honor them in all of their complexities. And as we honor their passing, and the tragic mystery of mortality, show us that this

void is not a void, but a portal. Grant us solemn imagination for new forms of being after death, and comfort us as we give thanks for their life, offering up gratitude with these shared words:

We honor who they were to us—partner, parent, sibling, child, aunt or uncle, niece or nephew, grandparent or grandchild, auntie, friend, co-worker, neighbor. We hold space for them in particularity, knowing that each of us knew and loved a distinct part of them. Some of us cried with them, some of us danced with them, some of us learned from them, some of us formed them. Comfort us in the particularity of each bond.

Dust to dust—

May rest welcome them home.

We honor their humor—every joke, however corny. Every wordless smirk and side eye. The way they teased us and still loved us. The moments we rocked back with a laughter so fierce, no sound could escape. May the joy that found them in life be magnified in death.

Dust to dust—

May rest welcome them home.

We honor the full contents of their lives, including the pain. The people they grieved. Every insecurity or fragment of self-hatred. Their suffering, spoken and unspoken, those secret heartaches that we will never know. And we ask that any injustice they endured that was not righted in life would be made right in death. That any honor withheld from them in life would be met with an unabated affirmation of dignity in death.

Dust to dust—

May rest welcome them home.

As we acknowledge their full humanity, so too do we hold memory for their flaws. For apologies never spoken, may they find remorse.

For wrongs not forgiven, may they find self-compassion.
Dust to dust—
May rest welcome them home.

We honor their labor. Years given to work, in contribution to a world that didn't always provide for them. We thank you for their service, for the things they elected to do out of care for the vulnerable, unconcerned for how it might profit them. We honor every choice made that honored the dignity of others.
Dust to dust—
May rest welcome them home.

God our maker, may the one we grieve find peace at last. Comfort us as we seek peace ourselves. May we learn how to continue living in their absence; may we uncover new forms for their presence. Let their death remind us of our own mortality, that we would live and love with awareness of the gift of each unpromised day. And as we stare into the portal of this passing, may we find beauty in our ending, however solemn that beauty may be. *Ase.*

NEW YEAR'S

Ancestors

Do not fall asleep in your enemy's dream.

—John Edgar Wideman

Wisdom

NEW YEAR

by Lucille Clifton

i am running into a new year
and the old years blow back
like a wind
that i catch in my hair
like strong fingers like
all my old promises and
it will be hard to let go
of what i said to myself
about myself
when i was sixteen and
twentysix and thirtysix
even thirtysix but
i am running into a new year
and i beg what i love and
i leave to forgive me

Dreaming

God of renewal,
We hold space for the sorrows and joys of another year. We have grieved. We have laughed. We have given too much and too little. As the year ends, ground us in the tension of remembrance and dreaming that this season holds. We remember all that we have survived, all that we loved and didn't love, and we honor it. There are those of us who feel ourselves inching closer and closer to our true selves, those of us who feel lost or aimless. Help us to honor our becoming without demeaning our past. Remind us that every season has its place, and that the path to liberation is never linear. As we peer into the new year, reorient us toward our desires and hopes, but protect us from dreaming as a form of self-loathing. May this be a season of so much more than heartless self-improvement plans. Protect our bodies from our own evaluations and judgment. Protect our souls from any guilt we carry for not becoming who we said we would by this time last year. When we toast to the new year, may it be emptied of self-contempt. May we meet our faces in new and old ways, stepping closer into ourselves in the years that come. *Amen.*

Breathe

INHALE: As it ends, I'll hold memory.
EXHALE: As we go, I'll hold hope.

LITURGICAL TEMPLATE
FOR ALTERNATIVE OCCASIONS

THERE ARE limitations to the liturgies contained in these pages. Namely, that I alone, with my particular voice and these particular hands, have written them. The danger of liturgy across time and traditions is that it has often been curated and preserved by a singular person, a task no one person can rightly be trusted to carry out. There are days you've lived that I could never speak to, longings and losses that I cannot fully understand.

To be liberated spiritually is to believe that you have a distinct and necessary connection to the divine, and are free to dream up new words and forms for that connection. For this reason, I've included a template below for the writing of your own liturgies—for other occasions and stories that resonate with you and the communities to which you belong. Not everyone will feel the need to pick up the pen. This is okay. But if you find yourself longing for more—for words that begin in you—remember, I am no nearer to the divine than you are, and my words no more sacred. Liturgy comes awake in the arms of the collective. This is my invitation. We get free together.

LITURGY FOR _____

Invitation

Words of welcome to ground the space. Who is gathered and for what purposes?

Ancestors

Select up to three quotations on a given topic from those who have come before us.

Wisdom

Passage of chosen literature that offers a teaching.

Truth-Telling

What confession or admissions can be named to bring one closer to the divine?

Mercy

What words of forgiveness can be spoken over the individual or collective?

Dreaming

Petition to the divine concerning your dreams and desires.

Breathe

INHALE:

EXHALE:

Departure

Closing words of blessing.

Acknowledgments

I ONCE thought that to be a writer I would have to protect my solitude above all else. I am grateful for each person who has reminded me that I am, in fact, held together by a collective. And that good words demand company. Thank you to:

The Black Liturgies community who has been so patient with me as I wrote this book. Three years ago, you asked for a book of liturgies, and instead received *This Here Flesh*. But you received it with all the care and celebration and advocacy I've come to expect from you. I hope this book was worth the wait. It contains so much of us. The phrases I'm most proud of are the ones that were held by us first. Thank you for showing me that the internet is not all violence, and not all strangers are to be feared.

The chorus of Black voices and ancestors whose words begin each section of the book. Any wisdom in my words began in you.

My literary agent, Tanya McKinnon, who is such a careful and dauntless steward of Black thought. Mostly, I just want to crawl inside your very mysterious and very alive brain. Thank you for choosing me.

My editor, Derek Reed, who knows when to fight for clarity and when to let my words be strange. Thank you for being so present to every word.

Lanecia Rouse Tinsley, who created an original art piece for the book's cover. Your work is generous and textured and honest. I'm learning from you.

My friends, who just keep calling. Who meet my long silences with unmerited endurance. Who respect me too much to idealize me. Yes, I've eaten today.

My family, by blood and by choice. Especially our newest borns, Wren and Charlie. I've been both born into and married into such chaotic and simple beauty. The older I get the more I just want to eat, and nap, and play spades and bridge with you while the kids scream. I wrote several of these letters in your presence, and they are better for it.

Shakur, who gave me the gift of hearing some of these words read in a child's voice. Who told me to come downstairs and play. Who told me to write something beautiful then give it away. You, next.

My husband, Wallace. *Can you believe it?*

References

Achebe, Chinua. *Arrow of God.* New York: Penguin Books, 2017.

Akṣapāda. *Living Toni Morrison.* Self-published, 2019.

Alexander, Elizabeth. *The Light of the World.* New York: Grand Central Publishing, 2015.

Angelou, Maya. *And Still I Rise.* New York: Random House, 2011.

———. *The Complete Collected Poems of Maya Angelou.* New York: Random House, 2015.

———. *Letter to My Daughter.* London: Virago Press, 2014.

———. "The Mask by Maya Angelou." Facing History & Ourselves, last updated May 2, 2022. https://www.facinghistory.org/resource-library/mask-maya-angelou.

Augustine. "Sermon 185." Accessed November 30, 2022. www.vatican.va/spirit/documents/spirit_20001222_agostino_en.html.

Baldwin, James. "The Artist's Struggle for Integrity." In *The Cross of Redemption: Uncollected Writings,* edited and with an Introduction by Randall Kenan. New York: Vintage Books, 2011.

———. "The Creative Process." In *Creative America.* New York: Published for the National Cultural Center by the Ridge Press, 1962.

———. *The Fire Next Time.* New York: Vintage International, 1993. First published in 1963 by Dial Press (New York).

———. "Go the Way Your Blood Beats." In *James Baldwin: The Last Interview and Other Conversations,* with contributions by Quincy Troupe et al. Brooklyn, N.Y.: Melville House, 2014.

———. *Notes of a Native Son.* New York: Penguin Books, 2017.

———. "The Precarious Vogue of Ingmar Bergman." *Esquire,* April 1, 1960.

Bambara, Toni Cade. *The Salt Eaters.* London: Women's Press, 2000.

Baraka, Amiri. "The Artist's Role Is to Raise the Consciousness of the People...." QuoteFancy. Accessed November 29, 2022. https://quotefancy.com/quote/2074805/Amiri-Baraka-The-artist-s-role-is-to-raise-the-consciousness-of-the-people-To-make-them.

Bennett, Brit. *The Mothers: A Novel.* New York: Riverhead Books, 2017.

Brooks, Gwendolyn. *The Essential Gwendolyn Brooks*. Edited by Elizabeth Alexander. New York: Library of America, 2006.

———. "Speech to the Young." In *BLACKS*. Chicago: Third World Press, 1991.

Butler, Octavia E. *Parable of the Sower*. New York: Grand Central Publishing, 2019. First published in 1993 by Four Walls Eight Windows (New York).

Clayborne, Carson, ed. *The Autobiography of Martin Luther King, Jr.* London: Abacus, 2000.

Clifton, Lucille. *The Collected Poems of Lucille Clifton 1965–2010*. Edited by Kevin Young and Michael S. Glaser. Rochester, N.Y.: BOA Editions, 2012.

———. *Good Woman: Poems and a Memoir, 1969–1980*. Rochester, N.Y.: BOA Editions, 2006. First published in 1987 by BOA Editions (Brockport, N.Y.).

———. *Next*. Brockport, N.Y.: BOA Editions, 1987.

Coates, Ta-Nehisi. *Between the World and Me*. New York: Spiegel & Grau, 2015.

Cone, James H. *The Cross and the Lynching Tree*. Maryknoll, N.Y.: Orbis Books, 2011.

Crenshaw, Kimberlé Williams. "It's Not About Supplication, It's About Power. . . ." QuoteFancy. Accessed November 30, 2022. https://quotefancy .com/quote/1698257/Kimberle-Williams-Crenshaw-It-s-not-about -supplication-it-s-about-power-It-s-not-about.

Danticat, Edwidge. *Breath, Eyes, Memory*. New York: Soho Press, 2015.

Dove, Rita. *Grace Notes: Poems*. New York: W. W. Norton, 1991.

Ellison, Ralph. *Invisible Man*. New York: Penguin Books, 2014.

Farmer, James. *Lay Bare the Heart: An Autobiography of the Civil Rights Movement*. New York: Arbor House, 1985.

Francis, Vievee. *Forest Primeval: Poems*. Evanston, Ill.: Triquarterly Books/ Northwestern University Press, 2016.

Gafney, Wilda C. "Love in the Wilderness." https://www.wilgafney .com/2022/04/03/love-in-the-wilderness.

———. *A Women's Lectionary for the Whole Church*. New York: Church Publishing, 2021.

Giovanni, Nikki. "Ego-Tripping." In *"Ego-Tripping" and Other Poems for Young People*. Brooklyn, N.Y.: Lawrence Hill, 1973.

———. "Poem for a Lady Whose Voice I Like." In *The Selected Poems of Nikki Giovanni*. New York: William Morrow, 1996.

———. *The Women and the Men*. New York: Harper Perennial, 1979.

———. "The World Is Not a Pleasant Place to Be." Weebly. Accessed November 30, 2022. https://nikkigiovannipoetryinfo.weebly.com/the-world -is-not-a-pleasant-place-to-be.html.

Gluckstein, Dana. *Dignity: In Honor of the Rights of Indigenous Peoples.* Brooklyn, N.Y.: powerHouse, 2010.

Hamer, Fannie Lou. "Nobody's Free Until Everybody's Free." In *The Speeches of Fannie Lou Hamer: To Tell It Like It Is,* edited by Maegan Parker Brooks and Davis W. Houck. Jackson: University Press of Mississippi, 2011.

Hansberry, Lorraine. *A Raisin in the Sun.* New York: Random House, 1959.

Hersey, Tricia. *Rest Is Resistance.* Boston: Little, Brown Spark, 2022.

Holy Bible: New Revised Standard Version (NRSV) Anglicised Cross-Reference Edition. New York: HarperCollins Reference, 2018.

hooks, bell. *All About Love: New Visions.* New York: Harper Perennial, 2018. First published in 1999 by William Morrow (New York).

———. *Appalachian Elegy: Poetry and Place.* Lexington: University Press of Kentucky, 2012.

———. *Killing Rage: Ending Racism.* New York: Henry Holt, 1996.

Hughes, Langston. *The Collected Poems of Langston Hughes.* Edited by Arnold Rampersad and David Roessel. New York: Knopf, 2007.

Hurston, Zora Neale. *Dust Tracks on a Road.* New York: Harper Perennial, 1991.

———. *Their Eyes Were Watching God.* New York: Fawcett, 1969.

Jones, Edward P. *The Known World.* New York: Olive Editions, 2017.

Jordan, June. *Some of Us Did Not Die: New and Selected Essays.* New York: Basic/*Civitas* Books, 2003.

Kincaid, Jamaica. *Annie John.* New York: Farrar, Straus and Giroux, 1997.

———. *The Autobiography of My Mother.* New York: Farrar, Straus and Giroux, 2013.

King, Coretta Scott. *Coretta: My Life, My Love, My Legacy.* As told to the Rev. Dr. Barbara Reynolds. London: Hachette UK, 2018.

Levy, Andrea. *Small Island.* London: Nick Hern Books, 2004.

Lewis, Robin Coste. *To the Realization of Perfect Helplessness.* New York: Knopf, 2022.

Lorde, Audre. *A Burst of Light: And Other Essays.* Foreword by Sonia Sanchez. Mineola, N.Y.: Ixia Press, 2017.

———. *The Cancer Journals.* San Francisco: Aunt Lute Books, 2007.

———. *The Collected Poems of Audre Lorde.* New York: W. W. Norton, 2017.

———. *The Master's Tools Will Never Dismantle the Master's House.* New York: Penguin Books, 1979.

———. *The Selected Works of Audre Lorde.* Edited and with an Introduction by Roxane Gay. New York: W. W. Norton, 2020.

Luchetti, Leita, dir. *Poetry Breaks: Lucille Clifton on What Poetry Is.* WGBH

New Television Workshops, 2016. Accessed November 28, 2022. https://poets.org/text/poetry-breaks-lucille-clifton-what-poetry.

Luscombe, Belinda. "10 Questions for Jamaica Kincaid." *Time*, February 4, 2013.

Malcolm X. "The Ballot or the Bullet." Speech delivered at King Solomon Baptist Church, Detroit, Mich., April 12, 1964. Political Sociology Course Readings, Middlebury University. https://sites.middlebury.edu/soan365/files/2013/02/Malcolm-X-The-Ballot-or-the-Bullet.pdf.

"The Martin Luther King You Rarely Hear." BLACK CENTRAL™, January 11, 2013. https://goblackcentral.com/2013/01/the-martin-luther-king-you-rarely-hear/.

Morrison, Toni. *Beloved*. New York: Vintage Books, 2004.

———. *Jazz*. New York: Vintage Books, 2004.

———. Nobel Lecture, December 7, 1993. https://www.nobelprize.org/prizes/literature/1993/morrison/lecture/.

———. "The Site of Memory." In *Inventing the Truth: The Art and Craft of Memoir*, edited with an Introduction by William Zinsser. Boston: Houghton Mifflin, 1999.

———. *Song of Solomon*. New York: Vintage Books, 2016. First published in 1977 by Knopf (New York).

———. *Sula*. London: Vintage Books, 1973.

NASB Grace and Truth Study Bible. Edited by R. Albert Mohler, Jr. Grand Rapids, Mich.: Zondervan, 2022.

"Negro Hymns and Songs: Spirituals. Lay Dis Body Down." In *A Library of American Literature*, compiled by Edmund C. Stedman and Ellen M. Hutchinson. 11 vols. New York: Charles L. Webster, 1891. Accessed November 30, 2022. www.bartleby.com/400/poem/1664.html.

Nichols, Morgan Harper (@morganharpernichols). "There is a reason the sky gets dark." Instagram, May 6, 2019. https://www.instagram.com/p/BxH7s5YA_ED/?hl=en.

NIV Study Bible. Grand Rapids, Mich.: Zondervan, 2011.

Rankine, Claudia. *The End of the Alphabet*. New York: Grove/Atlantic, 2007.

Rustin, Bayard. "When an Individual Is Protesting Society's Refusal. . . ." Goodreads. Accessed November 30, 2022. www.goodreads.com/quotes/9152-when-an-individual-is-protesting-society-s-refusal-to-acknowledge-his.

Sanchez, Sonia. *Wounded in the House of a Friend*. Boston: Beacon Press, 1997.

Shakur, Assata. *Assata: An Autobiography*. London: Zed Books, 2016.

Shire, Warsan. "For Women Who Are 'Difficult' to Love." Genius, 2014. https://genius.com/Warsan-shire-for-women-who-are-difficult-to-love -annotated.

Smith, Danez. "Say It with Your Whole Black Mouth." Academy of American Poets, 2018. https://poets.org/poem/say-it-your-whole-black-mouth.

Smith, Zadie. *White Teeth*. London: Penguin Books, 2017.

Taylor, Astra. "Cornel West: Truth." *Killing the Buddha*, November 15, 2009. https://killingthebuddha.com/mag/sinners-saints/cornel-west-truth/.

Thurman, Howard. *Jesus and the Disinherited*. Boston: Beacon Press, 1996.

————. *The Mood of Christmas & Other Celebrations*. Richmond, Ind.: Friends United Press, 1985.

————. "The Sound of the Genuine." Baccalaureate Ceremony, Spelman College, May 4, 1980. Howard Thurman Digital Archive, Pitts Theology Library, Emory University. Accessed November 29, 2022. https://thurman .pitts.emory.edu/items/show/838.

"Toni Morrison." *Charlie Rose*, 2020. https://charlierose.com/videos/31212.

Truth, Sojourner. "Life Is a Hard Battle Anyway. . . ." Historical Snapshots, November 24, 2020. https://historicalsnaps.com/2020/11/24/sojourner -truth-life-is-a-hard-battle-anyway/.

Tutu, Desmond. Foreword to *Dignity: In Honor of the Rights of Indigenous Peoples*, by Dana Gluckstein. Brooklyn, N.Y.: powerHouse, 2010.

Vendler, Helen. "The Art of Criticism." Interviewed by Henri Cole. *The Paris Review* 141 (Winter 1996).

Vuong, Ocean. *On Earth We're Briefly Gorgeous*. New York: Vintage Books, 2020. First published in 2019 by Penguin Press (New York).

Waheed, Nayyirah. *Salt*. Self-published, 2016.

Walker, Alice. *In Search of Our Mothers' Gardens: Womanist Prose*. New York: Harcourt Brace Jovanovich, 1983.

————. *Possessing the Secret of Joy*. New York: Vintage Books, 2009.

————. *Revolutionary Petunias and Other Poems*. London: Women's Press, 1999.

Ward, Jesmyn. *Men We Reaped: A Memoir*. New York: Bloomsbury, 2018.

Washington, Booker T., W. E. B. Du Bois, and Frederick Douglass. *Three African-American Classics: "Up from Slavery," "The Souls of Black Folk," "Narrative of the Life of Frederick Douglass."* Scotts Valley, Calif.: CreateSpace Independent Publishing Platform, 2016.

Wideman, John Edgar. *The Cattle Killing*. London: Picador, 1997.

Wilkerson, Isabel. *Caste: The Origins of Our Discontents*. New York: Random House, 2020.

Wilson, August. *Fences*. New York: Plume, 1986.

————. *Seven Guitars: 1948*. New York: Theatre Communications Group, 2008.

Woodson, Jacqueline. *Brown Girl Dreaming*. New York: Puffin Books, 2016.

Wright, Richard. *American Hunger*. San Bernardino, Calif.: Borgo Press, 1996.

Prayer Index

Permissions

Grateful acknowledgment is made to the following for permission to reprint previously published material:

About the Author

COLE ARTHUR RILEY is a writer and poet. She is the author of the *New York Times* bestseller *This Here Flesh: Spirituality, Liberation, and the Stories That Make Us.* Her writing has been featured in *The Atlantic, Guernica,* and *The Washington Post.* Arthur Riley is also the creator and writer of Black Liturgies, a project that integrates spiritual practice with Black emotion, Black literature, and the Black body.

colearthurriley.com
Instagram: @blackliturgies
Instagram: @colearthurriley
Twitter: @blackliturgist

More from
COLE ARTHUR RILEY

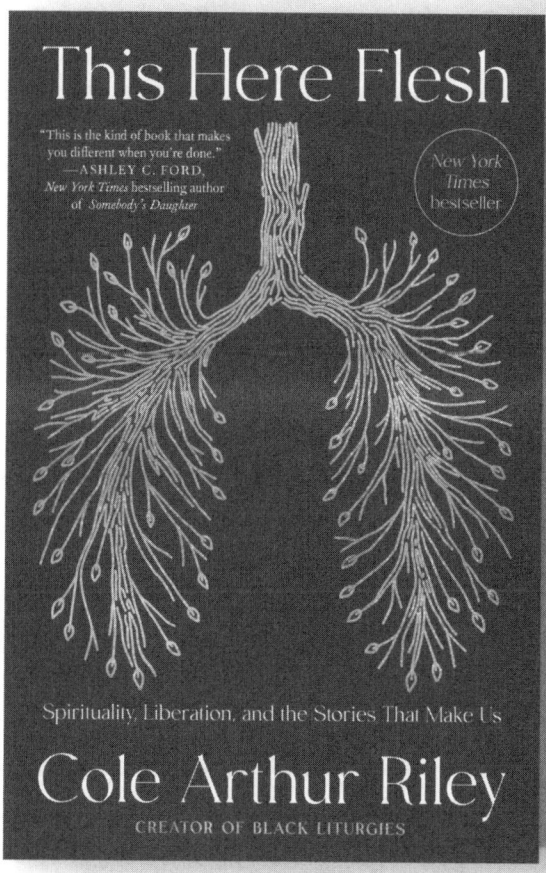

CONVERGENT

Available wherever books are sold